Grant's Campaign in Virginia, 1864 (The Wilderness Campaign)

Sawyer, George Henry Vaughan

BIBLIOLIFE

Copyright © BiblioLife, LLC

BiblioLife Reproduction Series: Our goal at BiblioLife is to help readers, educators and researchers by bringing back in print hard-to-find original publications at a reasonable price and, at the same time, preserve the legacy of literary history. The following book represents an authentic reproduction of the text as printed by the original publisher and may contain prior copyright references. While we have attempted to accurately maintain the integrity of the original work(s), from time to time there are problems with the original book scan that may result in minor errors in the reproduction, including imperfections such as missing and blurred pages, poor pictures, markings and other reproduction issues beyond our control. Because this work is culturally important, we have made it available as a part of our commitment to protecting, preserving and promoting the world's literature.

All of our books are in the "public domain" and some are derived from Open Source projects dedicated to digitizing historic literature. We believe that when we undertake the difficult task of re-creating them as attractive, readable and affordable books, we further the mutual goal of sharing these works with a larger audience. A portion of BiblioLife profits go back to Open Source projects in the form of a donation to the groups that do this important work around the world. If you would like to make a donation to these worthy Open Source projects, or would just like to get more information about these important initiatives, please visit www.bibliolife.com/opensource.

SPECIAL CAMPAIGN SERIES. No. 8

GRANT'S CAMPAIGN IN VIRGINIA, 1864
(THE WILDERNESS CAMPAIGN)

By
CAPT. VAUGHAN-SAWYER
INDIAN ARMY

WITH MAPS AND PLANS

LONDON
SWAN SONNENSCHEIN & CO., LIM
NEW YORK: THE MACMILLAN COMPANY
1908

CONTENTS

CHAP.		PAGE
I	OUTLINE OF THE WAR	3
II	PLANS AND DISPOSITIONS	19
III	THE WILDERNESS—FIRST DAY	33
IV	THE WILDERNESS—SECOND DAY	47
V	ADVANCE TO SPOTTSYLVANIA	63
VI	SPOTTSYLVANIA	79
VII	SHENANDOAH AND JAMES	93
VIII	NORTH ANNA	119
IX	TOTOPOTOMOY	139
X	COLD HARBOUR	155
XI	PETERSBURG	173
XII	FINAL OPERATIONS AND CONCLUSION	187

LIST OF MAPS

I	THE CONFEDERATED STATES	
II	VIRGINIA AND THE VALLEY	
III	EAST VIRGINIA	
IV	THE WILDERNESS—FIRST DAY	
V	THE WILDERNESS—SECOND DAY	
VI	SPOTTSYLVANIA	
VII	NORTH ANNA	
VIII	TOTOPOTOMOY AND COLD HARBOUR	

In pocket at end of book.

LIST OF AUTHORITIES CONSULTED

J. W. Draper.
J. C. Ropes.
A. Badeau.
H. Porter.
H. A. White.
A. A. Humphreys.
C. Baltine.
G. F. R. Henderson.
Wood & Edmonds.
Official Records.

GRANT'S CAMPAIGN IN VIRGINIA.

CORRIGENDA.

Page	10,	footnote,	*for*	Pope	*read*	Ropes.
,,	19,	line 1,	,,	H.	,,	U.
,,	38,	,, 21,	,,	Chewings	,,	Chewnings.
,,	71,	,, 12,	,,	Potomac	,,	Po River.
,,	74,	,, 16,	,,	Lee	,,	Meade.
,,	109,	,, 22,	,,	east	,,	west.
,,	110,	,, 4,	,,	east	,,	west.
,,	115,	,, 7,	,,	1,300	,,	13,000.
,,	120,	,, 21,	,,	, (comma)	,,	: (colon)
,,	190,	,, 4,	,,	Reans	,,	Reams.
,,	191,	,, 4,	,,	FitzHugh's	,,	Fitz Hugh Lee's.
,,	192,	,, 1,	,,	12	,,	28.

ERRATA.

Page	11,	line 13,	*for*	objective	*read*	objectives.
,,	11,	,, 26,	,,	was	,,	were.
,,	35,	,, 11,	,,	of	,,	on.
,,	57,	,, 9,	,,	combine	,,	combined.
,,	57,	,, 9,	,,	are	,,	were.
,,	67,	footnote	,,	his	,,	its.
,,	73,	line 18,	,,	was	,,	were.
,,	86,	,, 3,	,,	instruction	,,	instructions.
,,	102,	,, 5,	at commencement insert "it"
,,	156,	,, 14,	*for*	were	*read*	was.
,,	167,	,, 27,	,,	on	,,	in.
,,	179,	,, 3,	,,	he	,,	Lee.
,,	180,	,, 9,	,,	seems	,,	seem.
,,	184,	,, 20,	,,	number	,,	numbers.

OUTLINE OF THE WAR

CHAPTER I

OUTLINE OF THE WAR

APART from its own intrinsic value as a tactical study, this campaign has a special significance when it is considered in relation to the three years of indecisive struggle which preceded it. Thus a certain acquaintance with the course and nature of that struggle is necessary to fully appreciate the lessons of Grant's Campaign in Virginia.

Unfortunately, these preceding operations are very lengthy and complex. The campaigns were numerous and spread over a vast area. Their plans, objectives and fortunes were so varied and so constantly changing that it is not possible to give more than the briefest outline here. And in fact, although the study of the first three years of the contest is highly instructive, its value consists chiefly in showing how war ought not to be conducted.

The causes which led to the secession of the Southern States from the union were various and deep seated.

For many decades before the war there existed between the Slave Holding and the Non-slave Holding States of the Union social differences so great as to constitute them practically separate nations. They fell into these two divisions naturally, being sundered by complete divergence in feelings, pursuits, customs and political interests. The Northerners were mostly traders, manufacturers, and farmers and their wealth lay in the cities. Receiving nearly all the emigration from Europe, their political spirit was democratic, and the religious feeling inclined to be puritanical and intolerant. Almost the whole industry of the South and all their wealth were centred in the vast plantations of cotton and tobacco, and their prosperity depended upon cheap labour.

Causes Leading to War.

Already the Southern States suffered under hostile legislation. Free trade, which the planters needed, was denied to them by their Northern neighbours, and in several States there was a desire to secede from the Union years before the crisis arrived. In entering the Union, many States had stipulated a right to leave it in the event of Union being prejudicial to their interests, and this right, though not set forth in the Constitution, was held by the Secessionists to have been recognized. The Unionists argued that the right was invalidated by its omission from the articles, and quoted treaties with European Powers as proving the existence of an indissoluble Union. The Democratic spirit of the North predominating in the central Government gave rise to legislation unsympathetic to the South, and in the year 1860 the breach between the two sections had widened to complete estrangement.

The Abolitionists. Upon this field of dissension entered the Abolitionists—a violent hysterical party whose clamour was mistaken in the South for the voice of the Northern nation. They denounced slavery in extravagant terms and demanded instant emancipation of the slaves, regardless of the fact that the exchequer was unable to offer any compensation to the owners. At the same time there existed throughout the United States a large section of moderates who recognized the evils of slavery, but relied on time and civilization to effect its extinction. Their voices, however, were drowned by the yells of the fanatics, and the Cotton States, whose existence depended upon their slaves, believed themselves faced by ruin.

The election of Lincoln to the Presidency confirmed their fears, and immediately after, on December 17, 1860, the State of South Carolina declared its secession from the Union.

The legality of its action was not at once denied, but the Central Government declined to remove its garrison from Fort Sumter in Charleston Harbour.

As a sovereign State South Carolina could not suffer the presence of foreign troops in her borders, and after prolonged attempts at a pacific settlement had failed,

Governor Pickens bombarded the fort into surrender on April 12, 1861.

Outbreak of War and Secession of Cotton States. Meanwhile the Cotton and Gulf States, encouraged by the example of South Carolina, also passed Ordinances of Secession, and seized all the Government property and arsenals within their limits.

Between January 9 and February 1, 1861, there seceded the States of Mississippi, Florida, Alabama, Georgia, Louisiana, and Texas. They formed a Confederacy and elected Jefferson Davis of Mississipi, as President. As soon as it became evident that the North intended to coerce the Confederacy into reunion, four more slave States joined it, these were Virginia, North Carolina, Arkansas and Tennessee. The border States of Maryland, Kentucky and Missouri would also have joined, and the last two attempted to do so, but their proximity enabled the North to overrun them at the outset.

It will be seen, therefore, that the Southern States fought against what they considered an insupportable and tyrannical attempt to destroy their independence. The Abolitionist Movement was the torch which exploded the already overheated resentment against the North. There can be little doubt that civilization would in time have undermined the institution of slavery, and this war is one example among many of the hysterical sentiment of a few causing the destruction of thousands of lives and millions of money. In addition to this appalling waste, the Negro Problem in the States to-day is the legacy of the Abolitionists to posterity.

War was declared in April, 1861, and lasted four years. The white population of the North was 21½ million whites and half a million slaves. The South had 5½ million whites and 3½ million slaves, so that the whites were in the proportion of 4 to 1. To this numerical preponderance was added practically inexhaustible commercial wealth, and the command of the sea enabled the North to guard this commerce from interference, while at the same time they destroyed that of their rivals.

Probability of Foreign Intervention. The destruction of the commerce of the South, however, eventually reacted to their advantage, for as the war went on, the cessation of the export of cotton and tobacco began to be keenly felt in Europe. In Lancashire there was considerably widespread ruin. So the Richmond Government always hoped and believed that if they could only support the war long enough and with sufficient success they would obtain the first step to freedom. This was recognition by the Powers as belligerents, for in European politics they were always rebels against constituted authority. Such recognition would undoubtedly have been followed by intervention, at least, to open the ports and most probably to stop hostilities. In fact, in 1862 the Emperor Napoleon III was invited to invade and annex Mexico as an inducement to support the Confederacy and he was seriously considering the proposal. Such recognition and intervention would most certainly have been made before the end of the war, had it not been for the attitude of uncompromising neutrality of the British Government, and but for this attitude the States might not be United to-day.

With this hope of intervention always before their eyes the Confederacy strove to sustain a defensive war against its powerful adversary, and in this several circumstances aided them.

First, the Southerner was a better fighter, being an "out-door man," a horseman, and a hunter, as opposed to his opponent, who was mostly a townsman.

Military Qualities of the Combatants.

Second, they had from the start a leader of genius in General Robert Lee, and he was fortunate in two splendid Lieutenants, Jackson and Stuart.

Thirdly, the Generals who operated against Lee in the main theatre of Virginia were utterly inept, and their failures were assisted by the attitude of President Lincoln who, until 1864, insisted on keeping the control of the whole operations in his own hands. The Generals commanding the numerous armies were severally and separately responsible to the Cabinet, which set them to execute (under threat of dismissal) badly-devised civilian plans, and removed them from their commands in rapid succession as they inevitably failed. Under such a system of command it is not surprising to see the great Union Armies wandering aimlessly about fighting disconnected battles in immaterial localities and achieving nothing but defeat at the hands of the small but vigorous armies of the Confederacy.

The total forces ever enrolled by the South amounted to 600,000 men, while the North employed in the whole war 1½ millions, although nothing like those numbers were ever in the field at once.

Bull Run. The people of the North entered upon the struggle with almost light-hearted enthusiasm. Three armies of 50,000, 14,000, and 20,000 respectively were equipped for the invasion of Virginia, and as it was known that the South had only been able to raise about 35,000 men, an easy victory was expected to be followed by a triumphal procession to Richmond.

The long tale of the strategical errors of the war begins at once. The Federal Army of 14,000 sat in Maryland "covering the flank," the other, of 20,000, tried to threaten Virginia by operating west of the Alleghany Mountains; the main army alone was usefully employed in advancing to attack the Confederates at Bull Run and even here only two-thirds of it were employed in the action. The Confederates concentrated their whole force upon the invaders at Bull Run, and so signally defeated them that the 50,000 fled in rout back to Washington. No attempt, however, was made to follow up this victory, and the opportunity passed.

The Union Cabinet then bethought them that they needed a plan of campaign, and one was devised by Lincoln, Stanton, Halleck and McClellan.[1] Command was to be obtained of the Mississippi River to its mouth, thereby cutting off the extreme Western State of the Confederacy. The States west of the Alleghanies, Kentucky, Tennessee, and West Virginia were to be conquered, and their resources closed to the enemy. At the same time the chief effort was to be made by a large army under General McClellan upon Richmond, acting from a sea base on the peninsula between the James and York Rivers.

It is notable that the plan takes no concern with any of the Confederate armies, and it does not seem to have been established at that time that to make primary objectives of such things as rivers, territories and towns is fundamentally bad strategy and doomed to failure.

Tennessee and Mississippi. Part of this second plan succeeded. The States of Kentucky and Tennessee were wrested from the Confederacy mainly by Grant after several campaigns lasting one and a half years, and the last stronghold on the Mississippi fell in

---

[1] Stanton, Secretary for War; General Halleck, military adviser; McClellan, General-in-Chief. According to Pope the second was "careless, indolent and inexact to a degree hardly to be credited," and the last "a dreamer of confused and obstinate mind."

July, 1863, but the value of these successes may be judged by their absence of effect on the military situation in the main theatre.

The great expedition against Richmond after an unconscionable period of preparation was landed at Fort Munroe in April, 1862, and simultaneously a force invaded Virginia via the Shenandoah Valley

The Seven Days. Jackson signally defeated the latter in May and June, and then, combining with Lee at Richmond, drove McClellan's army in rout to their ships in June. McClellan's defeat was solely due to his attitude of mind, which preferred to slowly encompass inanimate objective rather than risk the fortune of a battle. His objective was the town of Richmond, and he resolutely refused to be diverted from it by any consideration of Lee's army, with the result that Lee fought him when and how he liked, and McClellan, who had come there to take Richmond, was not prepared for the contingency of a battle.

Thus terminated the second unhappy effort of the North. The third followed almost immediately, and was an invasion through the centre of Virginia by General Pope. His army consisted of all the Federal forces which had been wandering about Virginia and the Shenandoah Valley during McClellan's invasion, and to him also was sent some of McClellan's troops, though the majority of the latter were on the coast of the Potomac estuary at Aquia Creek.

Pope was a brave man but a singularly unfortunate General, and although he was largely superior in numbers, he was quite unable to cope with Lee and Jackson. Pope advanced to the Rappahannock River and really wished to attack, but was ordered from Washington to stand fast. As usual, the initiative was left to Lee. In August, 1862, he attacked the enemies' communications about Manassas Station with half his army, under Jackson. Pope fell back and attacked Jackson with the greatest determination, nearly overwhelming him. But he altogether failed to appreciate the situation, forgetting to take account of Lee, and that General, with the rest of his army, fell on the flank of the attackers, with such complete success that by the end of August, 1862, not a single Federal soldier remained in Virginia.

The Second Manassas.

It is to be noted that Pope was for aggressive tactics; but, unfortunately, he had not the quality of brain necessary to carry them out. He was one of the most unlucky of the Federal Generals, but by no means the worst fighter.

The Confederates now determined to take advantage of their enemies' disorganization and to carry the war into Union territory. It is to be remembered, however, that this was done not with any real hope of conquest, but to show to Europe that the Confederated States were able to maintain their independence and to establish thereby a right to recognition as belligerents.

Antietam. With this idea Lee invaded Maryland in September, 1862, and captured a force at Harper's Ferry, but being met by more than twice his numbers he was compelled to withdraw into Virginia after the Battle of Antietam (Sharpsburg) in which, although he repulsed the attack upon him, he barely escaped destruction.

Simultaneously with Lee's raid the Confederate Western army under Bragg advanced from Chattanooga to regain the lost States of Tennessee and Kentucky, but this effort was also met by greatly superior forces and repulsed after the Battles of Perryville and Murfreesburg.

Lee recrossed the Potomac in a somewhat parlous state, but there was no pursuit, and McClellan, who was again in command, followed him in a leisurely fashion until he was superseded by Burnside. Lee halted on the south bank of the Rappahannock, where Burnside attacked him in December, 1862, only to be severely repulsed in the battle of Fredricksburg. Nothing much was done in the winter and spring of 1863 except by **Fredricksburg. Chancellorville.** Grant, who was engaged in reducing Vicksburg on the Mississippi, but in May, 1863, the Federal army in Virginia, greatly reinforced and under Hooker, again attacked Lee on the Rappahannock, only to be utterly routed in the great battle of Chancellorville. The defeat of this fourth invasion of Virginia determined the Confederates to make a second and greater raid into the Northern States.

Lee invading Maryland with an army of 105,000 men attacked the Federal army (now withdrawn from Virginia to cover Washington) at Gettysburg in July, 1863, but was so severely repulsed that he had to again fall back, greatly weakened, into Virginia.

Gettysburg.

The Federal army, now under General Meade, again followed in an irresolute, dilatory fashion and, on Lee taking up a position on the Rapidan River, Meade halted facing him on the opposite bank. Detachments from both armies were then sent to reinforce their respective sides at Chattanooga, in which theatre the Federal Rosecrans had compelled Bragg to abandon that town and to retreat into North Georgia. Bragg on receiving the reinforcement of Longstreet's corps attacked and routed the aggressors at the Battle of Chikamauga on September 19, 1863, and driving them back into Chattanooga besieged them there.

Grant was then given command of the Federal Western Armies, and in November moved against Bragg, raising the siege and defeating him in the battle of Chattanooga on November 24, 1863. The attempt to pursue this advantage into Georgia was checked.

Chattanooga.

Meanwhile, Lee had been holding Meade in check by threats on his lines of communication, and so great was the apprehension caused by any move of his that he had no difficulty in keeping the army of the Potomac fully occupied till the end of the year 1863. The winter, as usual, precluded military operations.

At this period President Lincoln, realizing at last that a war cannot be successfully conducted by a Cabinet, handed over the complete control of all military operations to Grant and the campaign with which we are concerned commenced.

For the study of the campaign it is sufficient to remember, after reading this chapter, that the Federals, though they were vastly superior in men and in every kind of resource and had command of the sea, yet failed for three years to subdue their weaker opponents for the following reasons:

1. They made for their objectives territories, towns and rivers, and did not concentrate their efforts upon the main army of the enemy.

2. Their war was conducted by politicians without military knowledge.

3. They were singularly unfortunate in their Generals, while the South was led by men of genius.

6. The Southerner was a harder man and a more vigorous fighter and

5. Lee had the interior lines.

Other reasons also may be assigned, but these are the fundamental ones, and the first outweighs all the others.

PLANS AND DISPOSITIONS

CHAPTER II

PLANS AND DISPOSITIONS

ON March 9, 1864, H. S. Grant was commissioned Lieutenant-General and appointed to the command of all the armies of the Union. He proceeded at once to lay plans for a general, simultaneous advance. For this last and greatest invasion the forces of the North had been largely increased. The total enrolled at this time is given at over 660,000. The bulk of the Confederate forces were in two armies; one under Lee of about 70,000 in North Virginia, and the other under J. E. Johnston, about 60,000, in North Georgia. There was a force of about 5,000 under Breckenridge in the Shenandoah Valley and a division in the south-west corner of Virginia guarded an approach via the Kanawha River. Richmond was defended by about 10,000, and there were small garrisons in some of the coast towns.

Grant's Plan for May, '64. Grant's plan of campaign was as follows. The army of the Potomac, 140,000 men under Meade, was to move against the army of Virginia. Butler with 33,000, was to land on the south bank of the James estuary to affect a lodgment if possible in the Richmond defences, and if Lee fell back into the city the Potomac army would join Butler's forces on the James "preferably above the city" (Grant).

Crook and Averill with 10,000 from West Virginia were to advance up the Kanawha Valley to break the Tennessee-Virginia Railway, and thence to turn towards Staunton, where they were to make a junction with an army of 7,000 under Sigel, who was to have marched down the Shenandoah Valley. This combined army was then to move on to Lynchburg and thereafter return *via* Gordonsville to rejoin the Potomac Army, damaging roads and rails en route. Meanwhile Sherman with 99,000 was to advance from Chattanooga into Georgia against the army of Johnston. There was also to be an expedition of 30,000 under Banks to the town of Mobile near the mouth of the Mississippi.

Throughout the war the tendency of the Federals had been to employ too many forces on diverse objectives, and even Grant's plan seems unnecessarily extensive.

The James Expedition. With Butler's force Grant had great hopes of intercepting the southern communications of Richmond and establishing a blockade along the south bank of the James opposite the city. This proved to be impracticable. But

> Butler failed but better that he did?

PLANS AND DISPOSITIONS

even if Butler had succeeded in seizing such a position he could not have held it if the army of the Potomac had suffered reverse. In fact, in this event Butler's force would have inevitably been lost, for as it was reinforcements were brought against him, and he was blockaded on a small peninsula between rivers, and his whole force neutralized. Therefore it must be allowed that Butler might have done more good with the army of the Potomac.

West Virginia and Valley Expeditions. Of the excursions of Crook and Sigel, Grant himself admits that he did not expect much. They were intended partly to prevent the Confederates from drawing on the supplies of the Valley, partly to guard against the raids northwards through the Valley, of which the Washington Government had grown so apprehensive, but mostly to engage the Confederate garrison of the valley which might have gone to reinforce Lee. Now while Grant was attacking Lee in the open field the latter could not spare a man for raids, but as soon as he reached the Richmond works with an undefeated army he was able at once to send out a strong column through the valley which defeated the forces there and gained within three miles of Washington. Therefore, although Crook and Sigel did actually divert a certain force, it was a force considerably inferior to their own, and it would seem that they might have been better employed in attempting to crush the army of

Virginia before it gained the shelter of its works about Richmond.

Butler, Crook and Sigel would have added over 50,000 men to the Potomac Army, which might easily have turned the balance in the closely contested fighting in the Wilderness and at Spottsylvania Court House.

Banks's expedition to Mobile was a political move for which Grant cannot be held responsible. It was mere waste, although he exhibited much interest therein.

The Atlanta Campaign. Sherman's campaign, however, is to be carefully considered in relation to the main move. Each step of it was resisted by Johnston's army of 60,000, but the Atlanta campaign, brilliant as it was, was only of value to the issue of the war in that it occupied the army of Johnston. Sherman forced his way irresistibly to the heart of the Cotton States, destroying their capital and doing immense damage. But let it be supposed that Johnston's army had, ignoring Sherman, been conveyed to Virginia to double Lee's force, then it is clear that no amount of damage that Sherman might do to railways and cities would have aided Grant in Virginia, for Sherman could not have followed Johnston. With Grant's defeat Butler's force would have been lost and Lee could have proceeded to deal with Sherman if necessary.

The Army of the Potomac. So we see that Grant's campaign with the 140,000 men of the army of the Potomac was the only really material operation in which the 660,000 Federal troops were engaged and likewise that on Lee's army of Virginia alone depended the fate of the South. It was of no matter to the Confederacy even if every city in south and west had been devastated, provided only that they could have defeated the army of the Potomac.

However, Grant appears to have considered that 140,000 was a sufficient superiority over 70,000 to ensure success over Lee, and therefore indulged in what may colloquially be termed " side shows." And of course the final result is his justification. But it is to be considered that had Grant surrounded or destroyed Lee's army in the field in this campaign, the war must have ended then, and would not have been prolonged another year.

Confederate Strategy. With regard to the Confederate strategy, this was in the hands of President Davis, for Lee was not appointed commander-in-chief until 1865, when the cause of the South was already lost.

Throughout this campaign the army of Johnston in the Cotton States was resisting the advance of Sherman towards Atlanta, which although it was the commercial centre of those states, was a comparatively unimportant place when compared with Richmond or Petersburg. Atlanta was taken and destroyed in August, 1864, and in September, 1864, when Grant had firmly established his siege works before Petersburg, the majority of Johnston's army was despatched under Hood to make a raid into Tennessee in rear of Sherman, who was left to work his will in the Cotton States.

Had these tactics been employed four months earlier, and had Hood, instead of marching to his destruction at Nashville, joined the army of Virginia in the Wilderness, the war might have resulted differently. The defeat of their fifth great invasion might have well persuaded the Unionists to abandon coercive methods, for the North was tired of the war, and there were many both in Washington and Europe who were already working for peace.

Lee's Position on the Rapidan. In the spring of 1864 the army of the Potomac lay in the fork between the Rappahannock River and its tributary the Rapidan, and the army of Virginia faced it on the south bank of the latter river.

Below the confluence the combined stream could only be crossed at Fredricksburg and as had been proved in December, 1862, that crossing could be easily rendered impregnable. The fords over the Rapidan, however, were numerous, but all were watched, and from Barnett's Ford to Morton's Ford were covered by Lee's army.

Lee's right extended to the Mine Run Stream, and from that point to the confluence of the rivers extends a forest some ten miles from west to east and some fifteen miles from north to south. It was known as the Wilderness and was very dense with much tangled

PLANS AND DISPOSITIONS 25

undergrowth. "The ground on which the battle was fought was intersected in every direction by winding rivulets, rugged ravines and ridges of mineral rock. Many excavations had been made in opening iron ore beds, leaving pits bordered by ridges of earth" (PORTER). Usually it was impossible to see more than a few yards in any direction, and in places it was absolutely impenetrable.

Lee's position extended from Barnett's Ford, to Morton's Ford and thence to the Mine Run Stream, along which he had a return entrenchment on the edge of the forest. There were several practicable crossings below his right which were not covered by him, being only watched by pickets. Of these the most suitable were Germanna Ford, Culpeper Mine Ford, and Elys Ford. All led into the midst of the Wilderness, so that it was impossible for a force using them to skirt the forest by moving further east through the more easy woods about Chancellorville, without risking the loss of its communications.

Grant's Lines of Advance. Therefore to turn the right of Lee's position Grant had to plunge through the heart of this tangled forest, in which his numerical superiority was discounted, where movement was extremely difficult and where the enemy might be met behind insurmountable obstacles. But this route, bad as it was, had advantages, for by taking it Grant became independent of the railway.

Once he interposed between Lee and Fredricksburg he could replenish his trains by short road and river communications with the Potomac and Rappahannock estuaries.

In order to turn Lee's left he would have had to leave at least a corps to guard the railway, as that would have been his only source of supply. He would, moreover, have had to move in open country over the Cedar Mountain and other continuations of the South West Mountains in full view of the enemy, who would have had ample time to prepare for him. Also, he would forfeit all chance of driving Lee away from Richmond.

The fords into the Wilderness could be surprised, and Grant had some hopes of being able to emerge from the forest before being intercepted. Therefore, he decided on the Wilderness route.

In March, 1864, Meade, who commanded the army of the Potomac, reconstituted it, converting its five existing corps into three. These became the II, V, and VI Corps. The IX Corps (Burnside's), then on the railway, joined the army during the battle of the Wilderness.

The reduction of the number of corps was adversely criticized by some authorities at the time on the ground that in such enclosed country the difficulties of command would be increased. This view has some support in the situation of Hancock commanding the II Corps on the second day of the Wilderness fight. He found himself directing his own corps, one division of the V, a division of the VI, and a division of the IX. He had to assign his two wings to two of his divisional commanders, thus putting them over divisions of other corps to whom they were strangers.

Strength Returns. A tabulated statement of the organization of both armies with approximate strengths will be found following this chapter. These strengths, especially those of the Confederates, have never been accurately determined, nor is it possible to make a comparison of the returns on account of their irregularity and of the difference in the methods of preparation.

In the Union Army every man drawing pay was returned to tally with pay rolls, and included men not actually in the ranks.

The Southern soldiers were so seldom paid at all that there was not the same insistence on accuracy, and usually only men in the ranks were counted. At the close of the war the documents of the Confederate side dealing with the war were very defective so the question of their strength and losses will always remain in doubt.

Disposition of Armies, May, '64. At the end of April the army of the Potomac was disposed about Culpeper Court House. The II Corps, near Stevensburg, the V, two miles south of the Court House, and the VI near Welford's Ford. The IX Corps guarded the railway as far back as Bristoe station. The cavalry screened the front.

The headquarters of the army of Virginia was at Orange Court House, and the position prepared to defend the river lay from Barnett's Ford on the left to the Mine Run stream on the right, and up that stream to its source. It extended eighteen to twenty miles, and was watched by a few brigades of Infantry and Cavalry pickets.

To Hill's Corps was assigned the left, and to Ewell's the right. Both corps lay near the Orange Court House.

Longstreet's Corps was at Gordonsville. Of this Corps Pickett's Division was absent south of Petersburg. The main body of Stuart's Cavalry were quartered at Fredricksburg on account of forage facilities existing there.

It is to be noted that the divisions in these armies only numbered from 8,000 to 5,000 men, and sometimes less. The brigades varied from 3,000 to 1,500, and reference is at times made to "brigades" of 250 men.

ARMY OF POTOMAC

II Corps. Hancock Divisions { Barlow. / Gibbon. / Birney / Mott [1]

V Corps. Warren ,, { Griffin. / Robinson [1] / Crawford / Wadsworth (Cutler)

VI Corps. Sedgwick. (later Wright). ,, { Wright. (Russell) / Getty. / Ricketts

- Distributed among the other divisions about 10th May.

PLANS AND DISPOSITIONS

IX Corps. Burnside. Divisions { Stevenson. (Crittenden) / Potter. / Willcox. / Ferrero.

Cavalry. Sheridan. ,, { Gregg. / Torbert. / Wilson.

{ Infantry, about 120,000
Artillery, ,,   8,000
Cavalry   ,,   10,000
     Total   138,000 [1]
     Guns 316

ARMY OF NORTH VIRGINIA

I Corps   Longstreet. Divisions { Field. / Kershaw. / (Pickett absent on James).
(later Anderson)

II Corps. Ewell. ,, { Early. / Johnson (Gordon). / Rodes.

III Corps   A. P. Hill. ,, { Anderson (Mahone). / Heth. / Wilcox.

Cavalry. Stuart. ,, { FitzHugh Lee. / Wade Hampton.

Infantry, 49,000
Artillery, 4,800
Cavalry,   8,000
   Total   61,800 [2]
   Guns 224

[1] Draper gives 140,000 Federals and Union estimates give over 70,000 Confederates.

[2] Distributed among the other divisions about 10th May.

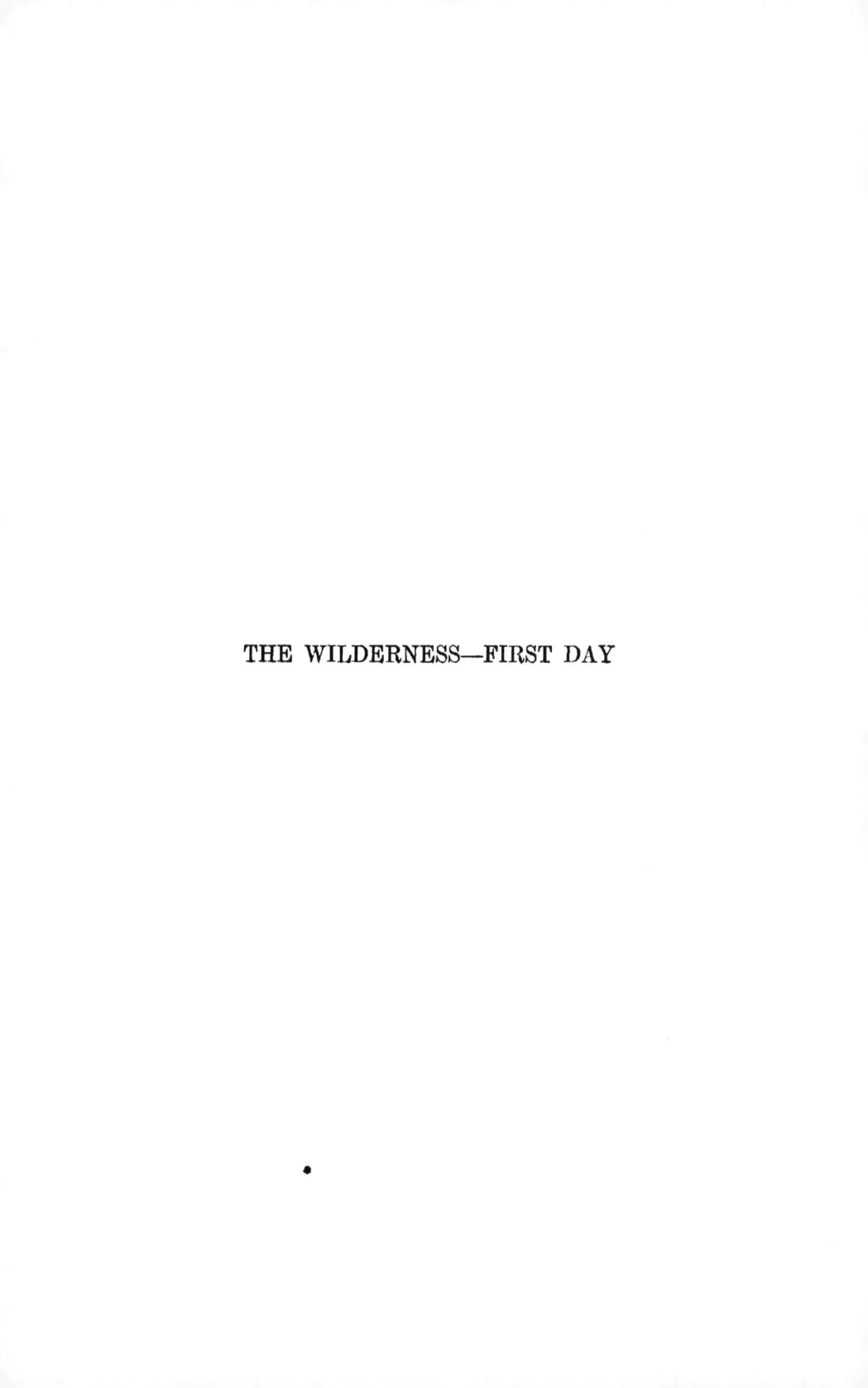

THE WILDERNESS—FIRST DAY

CHAPTER III

THE WILDERNESS—FIRST DAY

GENERAL MEADE, commanding the Army of the Potomac,[1] received the order to advance late on May 2, 1864, and his Infantry moved at midnight the 3rd–4th. The late hour was chosen in order that the preparations for the move might not be observed by the Confederate signal posts on Clarke Mountain, an eminence on the south bank of the river, about the centre of Lee's position The Cavalry Corps preceded the Infantry and had no difficulty in seizing the fords leading into the Wilderness, which were only watched by pickets. Five pontoons were laid before morning; two at Germanna Ford, one at Culpeper Mine Ford, and two at Elys Ford

The work was completed and the Cavalry had crossed to the south bank by 6 a.m. It does not appear, however, that Sheridan made any attempt that day to establish contact with the enemy, who was known

---

[1] The IX Corps was not brought under Meade's command until later.

to be to the west or south-west. The first contact was made unexpectedly by the infantry moving on the 5th.

<small>Federal Moves, May 4.</small> About noon, on May 4, the V Corps, followed by the VI, crossed at Germanna Ford; the II crossed at Elys Ford somewhat earlier. The trains used the Culpeper Mine Ford and Elys Ford.

The IX Corps had remained on the railway, and it is to be observed that although Grant had decided to abandon the rail as a line of supply, still he hesitated to uncover it until he knew definitely that Lee was moving against Meade. This illustrates the value of a reputation for aggressive activity. To leave Burnside behind was of very doubtful wisdom, for if Lee had moved up the railway in force, as Grant evidently feared he might, Burnside might have fallen a victim. If the rail was to be abandoned and Lee attacked, there was no use in leaving part of the force behind where it could accomplish nothing, and risking its being too late to assist in the battle, as might easily have happened. As it was, this concession to Lee's reputation for enterprise did actually deprive Meade of the support of the IX Corps on the 5th, and probably saved Lee from defeat on that day.

However, Grant, by a fortunate accident, obtained the information for want of which he was detaining Burnside. A signal message to Ewell from one of his brigadiers was read and deciphered about 1 o'clock on

THE WILDERNESS—FIRST DAY

the 4th, which revealed that Lee's Army was moving against the Wilderness. Orders were immediately sent to the IX Corps to make a forced march and join Meade without delay.

The V Corps reached the Wilderness Tavern on the afternoon of the 4th, and the II Corps arrived at Chancellorville rather earlier, at which places they halted and bivouacked. They might have gone considerably further, but it was thought unsafe to uncover the trains, which made slow progress, and were not all over the fords until 5 p.m. of the 5th.

The VI Corps was left covering Germanna Ford, pending the arrival of the IX Corps.

Confederate Moves, May 4. In spite of Meade's precautions his move was reported soon after he left Culpeper, and Lee at once put his troops in motion. He had, east of Orange Court House, Ewell's Corps, two detached brigades and two divisions of Hill's Corps. These troops moved on the Wilderness forthwith, Ewell by the Orange Turnpike Road, and Hill by the Orange Plank Road. Anderson's Division of Hill's Corps was on the Rapidan Heights north-west of the Court House and Longstreet's Corps was at Gordonsville. These were instructed to follow in haste.

Ewell and Hill were both informed that a general engagement was to be avoided if possible until the advent of Longstreet and Anderson. Longstreet should have arrived on the afternoon of the 5th, but in trying to make a short cut he lost his way and did not arrive till the morning of the 6th. Anderson, who had started later, came up about the same time.

On the night of the 4th, Hill halted seven miles West of Parker's Store on the Plank Road, with his outposts at the Store.

Ewell's outposts bivouacked on the Turnpike Road, within three miles of the Wilderness Tavern (where the V Corps lay) and his main body was some two miles behind them.

The Federal Commanders remained in ignorance of the proximity of both these bodies until the next morning at 7 or 8 a.m. The first was discovered by Wilson's Cavalry and the second by Warren's Infantry, and when it is recollected that the Federal Cavalry had crossed the river twenty-four hours previously, it is much to be wondered at that no patrols were sent down the Plank and Turnpike Roads during the 4th. These must have located both Ewell and Hill on that day, and the information would have been invaluable to Grant.

Dispositions May 4. Thus on the night of May 4, the Federal dispositions were as follows : V Corps at Wilderness Tavern ; II Corps at Chancellorville ; VI Corps at Germanna Ford ; IX Corps en route Elys Ford.

Of Lee's Army, Ewell's Corps was on the Turnpike five miles west of Wilderness Tavern, Hill's Corps was on the Plank Road, seven miles west of Parker's Store, and Longstreet and Anderson were en route to join Hill.

THE WILDERNESS—FIRST DAY

In the battle which followed, although most of the attacking was done by the Federals, Lee was, in fact, the aggressor. Grant's desire was to get clear of the Wilderness and fight where he could employ to the full his great numerical superiority, while Lee was determined to profit by Grant's difficulties. A few days previously at a conference of officers Lee had anticipated that Grant would cross where he did, and had expressed satisfaction at his entering the Wilderness. He hoped, no doubt, to deal with him as he had dealt with Hooker at Chancellorville, and set out to attack him while on the move and impeded by the dense growth of the forest. But Grant, although he would have preferred more room, had no intention of refusing a fight, as is shown in his order to Meade, issued early on the 4th. This is in somewhat colloquial terms and reads : " If any opportunity presents itself of pitching into a part of Lee's Army, do so without giving time for dispositions."

Federal Advance, May 5.
Grant's orders for May 5 indicate that he expected to emerge from the Wilderness on the south-west and meet Lee on the outskirts. The troops were ordered to move at 5 a.m. ; the V Corps from Wilderness Tavern to Parker's Store ; the VI Corps from Germanna Ford to Wilderness Tavern, and the II Corps from Chancellorville to Shady Grove Church, extending its right towards the V Corps.

Wilson's Cavalry Division was to reconnoitre towards Parker's Store and southwards, while Gregg and Torbert endeavoured to locate Stuart towards Fredericksburg.

On the Confederate side, Ewell and Hill, waiting for Longstreet and Anderson, were to stand fast.

Early on the 5th, Warren (V Corps) in advancing from Wilderness Tavern threw out Griffin's Division on his right to move westward along the Turnpike Road, while his other three divisions—Crawford's, Wadsworth's and Robinson's—pursued the more direct route on Parker's Store, which lay south-west. At about 6 a.m. Griffin encountered Ewell's outposts, who fell back.

First Contact, May 5.
The report reached Meade about 7 a.m., and he ordered Warren to halt and attack. Communication being difficult, the order did not reach the troops till 9 a.m., by which time Warren's leading division, Crawford's, was within a mile of Parker's Store, with Wadsworth and Robinson's Divisions following. Crawford took up a strong position where he found himself, at Chewings Farm, in open ground with a good command.

Wadsworth and Robinson began to form facing West, and attempted to connect up with Griffin, but the undergrowth here was very dense and their movements were greatly impeded.

At 7 a.m., on the receipt of the news of Griffin's contact, Grant ordered the II Corps, who were advancing

THE WILDERNESS—FIRST DAY

from Chancellorville, to halt and await events while Warren cleared up the situation; for Griffin's report was the only information he had, and for all the news his Cavalry had brought him Lee's whole force might have been falling on his right rear.

However, about 9.30 a.m. a report came in from Wilson's Cavalry that the enemy's Infantry had been located at Parker's Store at about 8 a.m. This indicated the whereabouts of Hill's Corps, and perhaps Longstreet's also, for although Meade was aware that the latter had been at Gordonsville, he did not know that he had not joined. Thereupon the II Corps, which had been halted for two hours two miles west of Todd's Tavern, was ordered to move on Parker's Store.

Federal Dispositions for Attack. At the same time (9.30 a.m.) the leading Division of the VI Corps, Getty's, which had just passed the Wilderness Tavern en route from Germanna Ford, was ordered to move by the Brock Road to the Plank Road and along the latter on Parker's Store. The next Division of the VI Corps, Wright's, was ordered to take a crossroad through the wood to reach the right of Griffin's Division. The third Division of the VI Corps (Rickett's) had been left to cover the Germanna Ford pending the arrival of the IX Corps, and was not up.

Meanwhile, from 9 a.m. till noon the two centre Divisions (Wadsworth and Robinson) of the V Corps were struggling in the dense undergrowth to get into attack formation and to connect with Griffin, and they fared badly. It was impossible to see more than a few yards in any direction, and the troops so lost their direction that they faced nearly north, presenting their flank to Ewell's right. Here they were attacked by the brigades of Daniel and Gordon and driven back in confusion. Crawford on the left of the V Corps also sent a brigade (McCandle's) to connect with the centre, but this met the same fate at the hands of Gordon.

Defeat of Federal Right.

Meanwhile, Wright's Division of the VI Corps also got entangled in the wood and failed to reach the right of Griffin's Division till 2 p.m. So that at 12 noon Griffin assaulted alone, and with such success that he drove back two of Ewell's brigades (Jones and Battle) in confusion for a distance of over a mile. There he met Ewell's main body, and being outflanked and unsupported on both sides, was driven back to his original position, with the loss of 300 men and two guns. Here he managed to maintain himself, and Wright arrived on his right at 2 p.m., just in time to stave off an assault by two brigades from Ewell's left.

Crawford being isolated on the left of the V Corps was withdrawn, and with Robinson succeeded in forming line on Griffin's left with Wadsworth in reserve.

Ewell now faced Warren and Wright, and both sides threw up log breastworks separated by about 300 yards.

THE WILDERNESS—FIRST DAY 41

Hancock's Advance on Federal left 2 p.m. Meanwhile, Getty's Division of IV Corps from Wilderness Tavern, and the II Corps (Hancock's) from Todd's Tavern were, at 9.30 a.m., making for Parker's Store, and Getty, having the shorter distance to traverse, arrived first. About 11 a.m., Getty arrived before Hill and found the Cavalry outposts engaged with Heth's Division. He did not feel strong enough to attack, so waited for Hancock. Hill, who was waiting for Longstreet, also did not take the offensive, but ordered Heth to halt in front of Getty and sent Wilcox's Division to assist Ewell. Heth and Getty erected breastworks.

At 2 p.m. the leading divisions of the II Corps began to arrive and were disposed on Getty's left along the Brock Road. Birney and Mott's Divisions faced Hill. Barlow's Division was on the left, occupying some high ground, with a clear front and good command towards either flank and over a possible line of advance by a disused railway embankment on the left. The Artillery of the II Corps were placed here. Gibbon's Division was in reserve.

Grant, however, refrained from attacking, and in doing so undoubtedly lost a great opportunity. He seems to have been disturbed by his ignorance of the location of Longstreet's Corps, and doubtless feared that Lee had some design in withholding it. Moreover, Burnside (IX Corps) had been slow to move and was not yet within reach. As the afternoon wore on Grant learned that Longstreet's Corps was not yet up, and determined, when too late, to attack all along the line, in hopes of crushing Lee before Longstreet's arrival.

Wadsworth's Division of V Corps had been withdrawn and reformed, and was ordered to move to Getty's right and fall on Hill's left flank, which was obviously at some distance from Ewell's right But this division again got entangled in the dense growth which pievailed in this portion of the field, and did not arrive till nightfall, when it only reached Hill's skirmishing line.

Federal left attack 4.15 p.m. At 4.15 p.m. Getty's Division, supported by Birney and Mott's Division, advanced to the attack Later in the afternoon two brigades of Gibbon's Division (II Corps) were sent in, but the remainder of that division and Barlow's Division were not advanced.

To resist this powerful assault of three and a half divisions upon his one, Hill recalled Wilcox, whom he had lent to Ewell in the morning, and placing two of his brigades on Heth's right, struck Mott's Division on its left flank and drove it back some distance, but the assailants coming within reach of Barlow's Division were in turn driven back by a flank attack delivered by two of his brigades.

Fighting continued till dark (about 8 p.m.) in which Hill suffered severely. Had Hancock's attack been delivered earlier and with his full force, it is most unlikely that Hill could have withstood him.

Fighting on the Federal right. On the extreme left the only fighting was an assault by a Division of the VI Corps on Ewell's trenches, which was repulsed.

As a result of the conflict on May 5, the V Corps had been forced back a little, and Ewell was strongly entrenched in its front. Hancock had made no progress, but had entrenched himself behind a triple line of breastworks.

THE WILDERNESS—SECOND DAY

CHAPTER IV

THE WILDERNESS—SECOND DAY

THE second day of the battle of the Wilderness is of less value as a tactical study than is the first. Grant's opportunity of overwhelming Lee passed with the arrival of Longstreet, and any chance that Lee might have had of breaking through Grant's defence vanished with the advent of the IX Corps.

Grant, however, still hoping to destroy Hill before Longstreet's arrival, had ordered a general assault at dawn, while Lee saw his last chance of success in adhering to his original design of beating his enemy while entangled in the forest. Thus on the morning of the 6th both sides are found intent on offensive tactics, and the Federal numbers being neutralized by the difficulties of the terrain, the greatly inferior forces of the Confederacy were able to sustain an equal contest, and even established a slight advantage at the end of the day. The battle consisted in a powerful assault by the Federal left wing, which was driven in by a brilliant counter attack. An attempt to follow up this success was repulsed with great loss, and throughout the day a succession of furious onslaughts were delivered and withstood by either side along the whole line without any material advantage being gained.

Grant's Orders for May 6. Grant's plan for the sixth was in accordance with his favourite tactics of applying the maximum of force from the beginning. He ordered an attack along the whole line, exerting his greatest strength against the Confederate right.

The V and VI Corps (5 divisions) were to attack Ewell. Hancock's command (consisting of his own Corps with the divisions of Getty of the VI Corps and Wadsworth of the V Corps) was to assail Hill. Wadsworth was to make a flank attack on Hill's left, which was in the air.

Burnside with the IX Corps, who was to march at 2 a.m. from Chancellorville, was expected to arrive in time to join Wadsworth with two divisions, while one division (Stevenson's) was to be sent to reinforce Hancock's left. The fourth division of the IX Corps, composed of coloured troops, was held in reserve at Wilderness Tavern, and eventually reinforced the Federal extreme right.

The hour desired by Grant for the advance was 4.30 a.m., as he was particularly anxious to secure the initiative from Lee. Meade thinking 6 a.m. better for the troops, a compromise was made and the assault ordered for 5 a.m.

THE WILDERNESS—SECOND DAY

But an earlier rise than even Grant had contemplated was necessary to anticipate Lee, who attacked at 4.15 a m. His intention was to feint with his left in the hope of drawing the enemy's force to that part of the field by giving the impression that he was falling on his right rear, and thereby diverting attention from his own right until Longstreet's Corps was prepared to deliver what was to be the main attack. This was necessary because Longstreet was not yet up He had marched sixteen miles on the 4th, although he only started at 4 p.m.; on the 5th he had lost the road and had had to retrace his steps, only reaching New Verdierville in the evening, after marching all day. He was then still ten miles from the field of battle, and at 12 30 a.m. the 6th he started to join Hill, so his troops were not in a condition to deliver a general assault immediately on their arrival at dawn.

The action was commenced at 4.30 a m. by Ewell, who anticipated Sedgwick and Warren's attack. He gained some initial success, but insufficient to divert the Federal main assault. Hancock advanced at 5 a m. with four and a half divisions (Getty's, Birney's, Mott's, Wadsworth's and half Gibbon's) keeping Barlow's division and two brigades of Gibbon's in reserve. This powerful attack was more than the two weakened divisions of Hill could withstand; their whole front was carried and their right broken.

Hancock s First Advance, 5 a.m.

G.C.   E

Hill's men, for the very bad reason that they expected to be replaced by Longstreet's troops, had only put up light breastworks, so they were quite unable to resist Hancock's masses, as they suddenly rushed out of the morning mist to close quarters. But they fell back slowly, fighting most stubbornly, and it is to be noted here that a fortified farm, Tapps, on the Plank Road, was not lost throughout the day, although more than once almost completely isolated. Its retention was rendered possible by the surrounding woods and thickets, for had it not been obscured from the general view the Federals would undoubtedly have concentrated against and taken it. As it was, it served as a valuable " point d'appui " and broke up the enemy's advance.

About the same time Wadsworth moved to attack Hill's left. He was greatly impeded by the undergrowth, and being unable to outflank Hill's line, he became the continuation of Hancock's frontal attack

6.30. Arrival of Longstreet. Hancock checked. By 6.30 Hill had been driven back about three-quarters of a mile, and his right division (Heth) was in rout, but at the critical movement, just as Heth's right had given way, Longstreet's Corps began to arrive on the field. Kershaw's division was on the south of the road and Field's on the north. Anderson's division of Hill's Corps was close behind; part of his force joined Field and part was held in reserve The defeated regiments of Heth rallying on the leading brigades of Field

THE WILDERNESS—SECOND DAY 51

brought the II Corps to a standstill and even regained some ground.

The first period of the Federal main attack came to an end here. Both sides were glad of a respite in which to reform their disordered ranks and for about two hours there was an interval in the fighting.

About this time Stevenson's division of the IX Corps was arriving behind Hancock's left on the Brock Road, and Hancock was informed that the other two divisions of this corps under Burnside were ready to support him on the right. Consequently at 7 a.m. he ordered Gibbon, to whom he had entrusted his left, to bring up Barlow's division and the remainder of his own command into line. These had been held back in apprehension of an attack from that flank, and Grant himself not being able to account for the absence of Pickett's division of Longstreet's Corps (which was on the James River), had ordered Gibbon to keep a sharp lookout on his left along the Brock Road. The impression that the left was threatened was mainly brought about by the action of part of Stuart's Cavalry, who by the boldness of their demonstrations and the rapidity of their fire gave the impression of infantry, and induced Gibbon to keep several brigades in echelon on his left rear.

So Gibbon, as it turned out providentially for Hancock, feared to move Barlow from his strong position and sent only one brigade, which reached the left of the attacking line after severe fighting:

Hancock's second attack at 9 a.m.

A little before 9 a.m. Hancock resumed his assault with five divisions (Wadsworth, Birney, Mott, Gibbon, and part of Stevenson's Division). Barlow being occupied with the cavalry did not participate, and Getty had been relieved and placed in reserve.

Severe fighting lasted till 11 a.m., but the most gallant endeavours of the II Corps failed to make any impression on the now rallied and reinforced troops of Hill. Wadsworth attacking on the right was killed and his troops were severely repulsed. Burnside's two divisions got involved in that particularly tangled portion of the field and did not come into action till the afternoon.

Longstreet's Counter Attack.

During the morning Longstreet had observed the disused railway embankment which led past the enemy's left and saw in it a covered way under which he could gain Hancock's flank unobserved. He passed four brigades (Mahone, G. T. Anderson, Woffard and Davis) along behind the bank till they were opposite the exposed flank of the assaulting lines. At 11 a.m. these troops, springing from concealment, fell on Hancock's left which, to use his own expression, collapsed "like a wet blanket," and his lines fled in great disorder back to their original breastworks along the Brock Road. The remainder of Longstreet's Corps with Hill's right wing followed hard upon them down the Plank Road. But at the moment when Longstreet, at the head of the columns, was leading

THE WILDERNESS—SECOND DAY 53

them into position for an assault he fell shot through the neck [1] by a party of his own flank attack which had arrived at the Plank Road and mistook the approaching group for retreating Federals.

His fall caused confusion among the troops, and much delay was entailed by the transfer of his command to Anderson and Anderson's to Mahone. The disorder that ensued was such that Lee, who arrived to take personal command of that part of the field, ordered the assault to be postponed till the afternoon.

Longstreet's fall was undoubtedly disastrous to the Confederate chances of victory, for an assault at that moment on the demoralized troops of Hancock and Stevenson would have had a good chance of success. But it must also be remembered that Barlow's division was still in its strong position on the left of the Federal works somewhat in advance of the line, along the Brock Road. His troops were quite fresh, the whole artillery of the II Corps was with him, and some of Stevenson's troops with Getty's division were in reserve. So that the success of Longstreet's attack, even if it had been delivered at noon, was at least problematical.

Fighting on Federal right and centre. In the other parts of the field the fighting, though severe, had no important results. On the Federal right part of the V Corps were driven back some distance at about 10 a.m. and Ewell threatened to break through just about where

---

[1] He was thought to be mortally wounded.

Grant's headquarters were located on the Germanna road But he was not strong enough to pursue his advantage, and Warren succeeded in re-establishing his line about 11 a.m. The V and VI Corps were then ordered to strengthen their works and stand on the defensive with a view to sparing troops to go to the assistance of the left if necessary.

In the Federal centre Burnside's two divisions had failed to reach the enemy, and when he eventually came into action about 2 p.m. he was held in check by two brigades detached from Anderson and Field.

Lee's attack 4.15 p.m. At 4.15 p m. Lee delivered his delayed assault on the Federal left, and a most sanguinary conflict ensued. Anderson and Hill's troops attacked against greatly superior numbers with desperate courage. They were aided by the woods catching fire in front of the position, for the wind drove the smoke and flames into the faces of the defenders, rendering part of the position untenable. At this point the front line fell back in confusion, and the Southerners charging up gained a temporary possession of the breastworks. But the success was shortlived, for Hancock at once threw in some of his reserves and the burning parapet was retaken. It was here that many of the wounded perished in the flames of the burning forest.

This assault of Lee's had been so costly that he was forced to recognize the fact that Grant's position was impregnable to any force he could bring against it.

THE WILDERNESS—SECOND DAY

At 5 p.m. the Confederates fell back slowly to their original position across the plank road, repulsing all attempts to follow them up Fighting continued till dark without advantage to either side.

Earlier in the afternoon Grant had ordered a general attack at 6 p.m., but this had been anticipated by Lee's onslaught at 4.15, and by the time this was repulsed Hancock's men were exhausted and his ammunition almost expended.

Assaults by Burnside and Ewell. At the time that Lee's final effort threatened the Federal right Burnside was ordered to attack in order in relieve the pressure. But he was not able to do so till 5.30, when he delivered a very vigorous assault on Hill's left. Reinforcements, however, were brought from the right and Burnside was again repulsed.

During the day severe combats had taken place between the cavalry of the two armies on the Furness and Brock roads and at Todd's Tavern, but with no decided result.

Lee's final assault was the last material fighting in the day, except for a somewhat unaccountable endeavour by Early's division of Ewell's corps. This made a very successful assault late in the evening on the extreme right of the VI Corps, which was taken by surprise. Two brigadiers with the greater part of their brigades were captured, but the rest of the line stood firm and in the pursuit of the defeated troops the victors fell into disorder in the thick forest. Night ended the conflict.

The utility of this effort is difficult to see. It was entirely isolated, and had it even achieved greater success than it did there were no troops within reach to turn the success to account. Moreover, it came so late that even if it had been possible to support it the darkness of night in a dense forest must have put an end to all movements of troops.

Early's attack, however, caused the VI Corps to be withdrawn during the night into reserve and the right of the V Corps was bent back.

The two days' fighting convinced both Lee and Grant of the futility of further attempts to break through each other's positions, and on the 7th Grant made arrangements to move on to a locality more favourable to the deployment of his force.

The Federal losses during the two days of the Wilderness fighting are given at 17,600, while that of the Confederates is variously computed between 8,000 and 11,000. Some figure between the two is probably correct.

In reading the account of this seemingly equal contest it is apt to be forgotten that Lee was outnumbered by about 2 to 1.

Ewell's three divisions on the turnpike actually made considerable headway against the five divisions of the V and VI Corps, who were also supported by a division of the IX.

THE WILDERNESS—SECOND DAY

Hill with two divisions throughout the 5th had withstood the assault of three and a half divisions.

On the 6th Lee's right, consisting of five divisions, defeated Grant's left, which disposed nine divisions.

Causes of Federal Repulse. That eight divisions (of about 70,000 men) should have prevailed against fifteen divisions (of about 140,000 men) is a circumstance which arrests attention. The causes which combine to bring about this unusual event are various.

First, as Lee had anticipated when he ventured to assail such a formidable army, the dense forest in which Grant fought greatly hampered movement, while Lee's army on the outskirts was not so restricted. It will be observed on the 5th that the whole left of the V Corps met disaster from this cause, and Wadsworth's division when sent to reinforce Hancock on that day failed to reach him through the dense undergrowth. The same difficulty was experienced by the two divisions of the IX Corps on the 6th, and they also failed to reach the enemy in time to do any good. The impenetrable nature of the woods in the Federal centre alone enabled Hill and Ewell to hold their positions for they were widely separated with their inner flanks in the air. Lee was thus able to dispense with a centre and use his whole force on his two wings.

Another circumstance which aided Lee was the failure of the Northern cavalry to locate his army on the 4th and 5th, whereby Grant was unable to apply his great force on the first day of the battle On that morning Longstreet was out of reach, and Hill, with two divisions only, barred the Plank Road At the time when Hill should have been assailed, had his position been known to Grant, Hancock was several miles distant on the Pinney Branch Road wandering away from the field of battle. Had Hill been attacked at 8 a m on the 5th in the manner in which he was attacked at 2 p.m., there is little doubt that Grant could have emerged victoriously from the forest and he would then have stood a fair chance of cutting Lee off from Richmond. The fact that Hill was not attacked till the afternoon enabled him to lend half his force to Ewell in the morning to assist in the discomfiture of the V Corps.

To this failure of the Northern cavalry more than to any other cause must be attributed Grant's non-success in the Wilderness.

A brilliant contrast is the action of Stuart's ragged horsemen. Coming from Fredricksburg they passed close across the Federal front, defeating the attempt of two strong cavalry division's of Gregg and Torbert to intercept them. Throughout the 5th and 6th they not only held up the whole of the Federal cavalry along the Brock Road, but also effectually assisted the infantry by threatening the enemy's left. In addition to this they watched the Federal rear at Chancellorville, and immediately reported the movement of the trains on the 7th.

Lastly Lee had the advantage of better infantry than his opponent. They were by now all veterans of many fields, while a large number of the Northern troops were fresh. Their constant inferiority in numbers compelled loose formations with their consequence of increased individual resource and self-reliance. They had learned to thread the forest in single file and to form rapidly to the front when the enemy was encountered, while the well-filled Federal ranks strove to keep their line formations and were broken up by the thickets.

ADVANCE TO SPOTTSYLVANIA

CHAPTER V

Advance to Spottsylvania

By the morning of the 7th, Grant had decided against further attacks on Lee's works. The necessity of covering the march of his trains had passed as they were now well up behind the army, between it and Fredericksburg. So being no longer committed to the Wilderness, he was at liberty to continue his original intention of moving to his left until he could bring the enemy to battle on a field favourable to himself. Consequently he issued orders on the 7th to move the whole army to Spottsylvania Court House.

In abandoning the field of battle, however, Grant departed in some measure from his own professed principles of "never manoeuvring," and also from his own dictum that the army of Virginia was to be his primary objective. In relinquishing his positions and making for Richmond he entered into a marching competition with the Confederate army which had always proved itself the more mobile and thereby he accepted the probability that it would forestall him on his route towards

Richmond. His great opportunity lay in defeating that army, at a distance from its capital, in such a manner as to prevent it reaching that refuge In proportion as he transferred the contest towards the south-east so did he lessen his chance of terminating the war by inflicting irretrievable defeat on the main army of the Confederacy in the field.

A flank march under the eyes of an active enemy is always accompanied by risk, and Grant had not adequate reason to be certain that Lee would conform to his movement. If for the sake of argument we suppose that Lee had been able to obtain reserves or had obtained reinforcements and had pressed on, on the 8th, at Todd's Tavern, he would have taken the Federal army in a most disadvantageous position. With this consideration before us it might be useful to consider Grant's alternative and more regular course of continuing the battle of the Wilderness by resuming his attacks on Lee's right and by reinforcing them from his own right to have gradually outflanked it.

If he had been able to press round between Parker's Store and Shady Grove Church he would have been in a better position to interpose between Lee and Richmond than he was at Spottsylvania, and to intercept him Lee would have had to make a longer and more circuitous march with troops wearied by three or four days' continuous fighting.

As such a course would have been a more ordinary one,

it may be permissible to speculate on its chances and to compare it with that adopted by Grant.

For three days at Spottsylvania the Federal divisions delivered a long succession of the most gallant and desperate assaults on record upon a position far stronger than that in the Wilderness, and with secure flanks. Had these assaults been thrown on the unsupported right of the Confederates at Parker's Store it is likely they would have been more fortunate, and even had they been repulsed the Federal army would have been in a far better position strategically than it was after Spottsylvania.

Thus it may be said that Grant recoiled from the completion of his task in the Wilderness and sought to gain by manoeuvring what he had set out to gain by fighting.

On the 7th, nothing was done by the infantry of either side, but a severe struggle took place between the cavalries. On the 5th, Sheridan with two of his divisions encountered Stuart's brigades as they were returning from Fredericksburg to join the army, and some unimportant fighting took place. On the 6th, he had engaged them throughout the day three or four miles south of Chancellorville and succeeded in pressing them back, but with difficulty, on Todd's Tavern. On the 7th, being joined by Wilson's division, he again attacked them, this time with more success and compelled them to fall back,

Cavalry Actions, 5th to 7th.

Fitzhugh Lee's division southward along the Brock Road and Hampton westwards. He determined to pursue the advantage the next morning by pressing on to seize the crossings of the Po River, but this admirable intention was foiled by Meade, who countermanded Sheridan's orders and commanded him to protect the advance of the columns southwards.

The consequence was that on the night of the 7th Sheridan's regiments, being checked by obstructions, blocked the progress of the infantry columns, and this led to a violent quarrel between Sheridan and Meade, in which the former stated, in the vivid language for which he was noted, that if he were given a free hand he would undertake to demolish the opposing cavalry. Whereupon Grant acceded to his suggestion, and on the 8th Sheridan started to raid the enemy's communication with his whole force.

Move to Spottsylvania, night, May 7. On the afternoon of the 7th Meade's trains began to move off from Chancellorville so as to get a good start, and that evening the flank march to Spottsylvania commenced. The right was withdrawn first. The V Corps marched at 8.30 p.m. by the Brock Road, passing in rear of the II Corps. At the same time the VI Corps, which had already been withdrawn from the front line, proceeded via Chancellorville and the Pinney Branch Church Road, so as to arrive on the

ADVANCE TO SPOTTSYLVANIA

left of the V Corps. The II Corps was to follow the V, and the IX Corps was to guard the rear of the trains and follow the route of the VI Corps.

The first move of the Federal trains was observed by Stuart's indefatigable scouts, but the news had far to travel and only arrived late in the evening. At 11 p.m. Anderson's (formerly Longstreet's) corps was despatched to Spottsylvania Court House via Corbyn's Bridge and the Shady Grove Church Road. They marched all night, and in the early morning observing Warren's troops on the Brock Road they pushed on to forestall him at the Court House. This they succeeded in doing owing to the difficulties experienced by the V Corps on the Brock Road.[1] Soon after starting Warren was delayed by the baggage and huge escort of the head-quarter staff which occupied the road. Next he was blocked by his own cavalry, who were endeavouring, unsuccessfully, to clear the FitzHugh Lee's cavalry from the front, and eventually when they yielded the road to him he found his progress hampered by felled trees and other obstructions. It was then daylight and his advance guards came under the fire of Lee's dismounted troopers. These so delayed the leading division that it did not get in sight of the Court House until 8 a m on the 8th. So that by the time Warren's troops reached Alsop's Farm, two miles from the Court

[1] Wilson's cavalry division having made a detour to eastward had reached the Court House in advance of Anderson, but was unable to hold his ground.

House, thoroughly tired out, they found Anderson's corps entrenched on a ridge in their front.

Fighting on May 8. The V Corps, however, made a determined effort to dislodge Anderson and some sharp fighting ensued but the ridge being found too strong they desisted and threw up entrenchments 200 to 400 yards from the position.

On the arrival of the VI Corps in the afternoon the fight was resumed, but Ewell's corps arriving just in time took post on Anderson's right and the attacks were repulsed.

Meanwhile, Hill's corps (temporarily under Early) had been ordered to march via the Brock Road, getting on to it at Todd's Tavern. These orders were either a mistake or indicated that Lee wished Early to engage the troops which must have been expected to be met on the Brock Road. Early, endeavouring to carry out these orders, encountered the II Corps, which was halted at Todd's Tavern to protect the flank of the general advance. He remained before it throughout the day and night of the 8th, but only the outposts came in contact. It is not clear why he did not push on to join Lee at once. Probably he hoped Hancock might give him an opening.

Movements on May 9. At dawn on the 9th Early marched via the Shady Grove Church and took post on the Confederate right.

Hancock also advanced on the Brock Road and formed

ADVANCE TO SPOTTSLYVANIA

on the Federal right with three divisions; the fourth, Mott's, was sent to left of the VI Corps.

The same morning the IX Corps arrived on the Federal left and faced the right of Ewell's corps.

The 9th was spent by both sides in strengthening their positions and some skirmishing took place in which General Sedgwick, commanding the VI Corps, was killed. He was succeeded by Wright.

The Federal losses on the 8th and 9th are given at about 2,000.

During the 9th Hancock was ordered to cross the Po River with his three divisions to reconnoitre the Confederate left. As his presence there threatened the Confederate trains which were still marching on the south of the Po, Early was sent with two divisions from the right to oppose Hancock, but before any serious encounter occurred Grant had determined to attack the position in front and recalled two of Hancock's divisions on the morning of the 10th.

Barlow's division of this corps remained, and being assailed during the day by Heth's division was compelled to retreat the way it had come with considerable loss.

Lee's Position. The position on which Grant had determined to make a frontal attack was a strong one. It lay across the peninsula formed by the Po and the Ny Rivers, and has been described by different authorities in terms which vary a good deal. ⁱThe map is the best guide, but verbal terms are necessary to describe the action. The left of the position rested on the Po River and ran for about a mile slightly north of east. It then turned about north-east by north for about half a mile. This left wing was held by Anderson's corps ⁾ From here commenced the portion of the works known as the Salient or Bloody Angle of sinister fame. It consisted of a line of some 400 yards facing a little west of north, and this will be described hereafter as the west face of the angle. The works then began to bend southwards. For about 600 yards they presented a curve facing N.N.E., making the east face of the angle. Then they ran southwards. The two faces of the angle and about half a mile of their southern continuation were held by Ewell's corps and formed Lee's centre. The southern continuation of Ewell's position was held by part of Early's corps with part in reserve.

It will be observed that the true salient was formed by Anderson's left and Ewell's position, but the term salient is apt to confuse if it is applied, as it has been, to the broad angle at its apex, where the principal fighting occurred.

The west face of the angle was held by Rodes' division and the east face by Johnston's division, both of Ewell's corps.

On May 10 the Federal V Corps faced the centre and right of Anderson's corps. The VI faced Ewell's left.

ADVANCE TO SPOTTSYLVANIA

The IX Corps was opposite Early's left on the Fredericksburg Road.

Assaults, May 10. At 3.45 p.m. on the 10th, Warren attacked Anderson's centre with two divisions of the V Corps and half a division of the II Corps. (Crawford's, Wadsworth's under Cutler, and half Gibbon's.) The assault was made with much vigour and gallantry and in places actually reached the parapet; but the works were too strongly defended, and the V Corps was eventually driven back with very heavy loss. At 7 p m Hancock having returned from the reconnaissance across the Potomac was directed to resume the assault on Anderson's centre, which he did with the divisions of Birney and Gibbon, but with no better success. The attacks on Anderson's position appear to have been somewhat disconnected. Some writers mention as many as four; Gibbon at 11 a.m.; Crawford and Cutler at 3 p m., and two more in the evening by the V and II Corps combined In fact, the movements do not seem to have been as well timed as they might have been, considering that Grant clearly intended a general assault.

The co-operation of the VI Corps in the operation was confined to an attack of two brigades under Upton. At 4 p.m. these, taking advantage of a wood which approached the position, were able to form up within 200 yards of Rodes' troops and charging out at 6 p.m. carried two lines of breastworks. Mott's division of the

II Corps which had been placed between the VI and IX Corps was to have attacked at the apex of the angle simultaneously with Upton. But in trying to form for advance it came under a heavy fire from Johnston's artillery at the apex of the angle and was thrown into confusion. Meanwhile, Burnside with the IX Corps had been ordered to reconnoitre the enemy's right and prevent him from detaching troops to reinforce his centre. Burnside, however, could not make up his mind to attack without definite orders (PORTER), so he remained inactive, contenting himself with erecting works. Consequently Upton, being entirely unsupported, was unable to maintain his position and was ejected with heavy loss by Rodes' reserves. Grant was much dissatisfied with Burnside's failure, but it must be noted that his orders to the IX Corps did not indicate that he wished for a genuine assault from them. But on the other hand Grant sent a staff officer to Burnside, authorized to explain his wishes. This officer (Major, afterwards General Porter) urged an attack with three divisions, but Burnside insisted on again referring to Grant and the reply came too late.

The attacks on the 10th were very costly, the Federal losses being about 4,000. They served, however, as a reconnaissance in force, as they revealed the weakness of the apex of the salient. Grant was well satisfied with the result, and from Upton's success conceived hopes of yet being able to break through Lee's lines.

ADVANCE TO SPOTTSYLVANIA

Yellow Tavern. Death of Stuart.

While Lee was successfully resisting the Federal masses at Spottsylvania, that which amounted to a disaster overtook the Southern armies, for on May 11 Stuart made his last fight against the heavy odds which at last prevailed over all the valour and devotion of the South.

On the 8th, Grant despatched Sherman to raid the enemy's communications, and to make a trial of the Richmond defences 50 miles distant. He was to threaten Richmond and then join the army of the James, passing to the west of the capital. After that he was to cross the peninsular between the James and York Rivers to White House, destroying communications, and to rejoin Grant after having made the circuit of Richmond.

On the 9th he started with 10,000 sabres and moved round Lee's right. On the 10th the Virginia Central Railway was reached at Beaver's Dam Station about eighteen miles south of Spottsylvania and ten miles of track with some stock was destroyed. Next day he reached Ashland Station, thirteen miles from Richmond, and was destroying the line there when Stuart overtook him.

Three brigades of Confederate cavalry, about 1,000 sabres each, had followed on the 11th. Stuart, with two brigades, making a circuitous route reached Yellow Tavern (six miles from Richmond) heading the raiders off, while the third, under Gordon, hung on their rear, making them face both ways. Not having had time to put up defences, the small Southern force was unable to withstand the Federal corps of three times its numbers and although they sustained the conflict throughout the day they were eventually dispersed. Gordon was killed and Stuart mortally wounded. He was fighting in the front line and firing over his men's heads with a pistol.

But the delay thus imposed on the Federal columns served the end for which Stuart had fought, in that it gained time for the untenanted Northern works of the city to be manned. Sheridan pushing on penetrated the first line of defences, but was so severely repulsed from the second line that he was forced to abandon his project of joining the James army. Being pressed by the Richmond troops he had to fall back eastwards across the Chickahaminy and make for Haxalls Landing on the James estuary, whence he rejoined Lee a week later, moving by sea.

Excepting the fortuitous removal of Stuart and Gordon this raid accomplished nothing, for the damage to the rails was easily and immediately repaired. It would be instructive to know the number of horses which were broken down in it.

In principle it was thoroughly bad, and these pernicious tactics were frequently resorted to by both sides in the war. The fact that Stuart twice rode round the Federal army, and that other leaders on both sides made similar and very plausible manoeuvres, is no justification for the practice of detaching the whole cavalry of an army on independent excursions without a definite object, other than that of damaging communications If Stuart had not been detached in the Seven Days, Lee would have penetrated McClellan's intentions twenty-four hours earlier and might have destroyed his army. Stuart's absence at Baltimore during the battle of Gettysburg contributed largely to Lee's defeat there. Hooker at Chancellorville sent the whole of his cavalry to wait outside Richmond for the rout of Lee's army, whereby he remained in ignorance of Lee's movements and was himself routed. With these excursions is to be compared Forrest's raid on Holly Springs with a specific objective in the destruction of Grant's depots, containing the accumulated supplies for his advance on Vicksburg. The war is prolific in instances of the misuse of cavalry, as well as in fine examples of its proper employment, but it must be said that the more vivid exploits of Stuart's brilliant career which made his name famous to the public, were not those which earned him his great reputation among soldiers. Curiously enough all this was summed up undesignedly by Lee in his spontaneous comment on Stuart's death. On hearing the news he was overcome with distress, and after a brief disjointed formula of regret he exclaimed, " He never brought me a piece of false information!" That was the only eulogy bestowed by Lee on one whose courage and prowess in battle were famous in two continents.

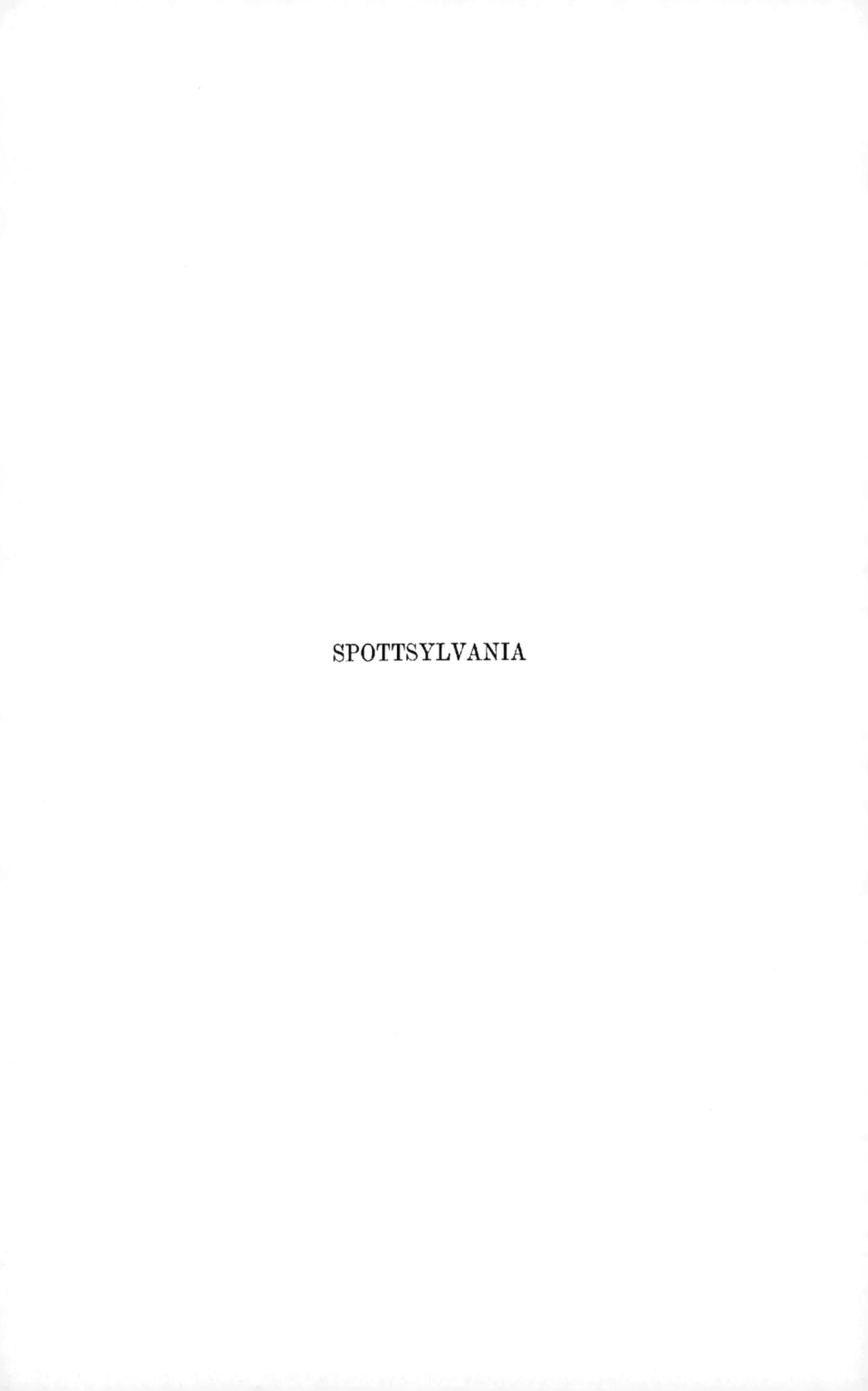

SPOTTSYLVANIA

CHAPTER VI

SPOTTSYLVANIA

NOTHING was done at Spottsylvania on May 11, but during that night the II Corps was transferred from the right and placed between the VI and IX Corps, opposite the apex of the angle. Orders were issued for an assault on the angle before dawn on the 12th. The II Corps was to form as near as possible to the apex and to attack at 4 a.m. The IX Corps was to co-operate at the same hour. The VI and V Corps were to be in readiness to assault the line opposite them or to reinforce the main attack as might be required.

Plan of Attack for May 12.

During the night of May 11 movements heard on the Federal right led Lee to imagine that an attack was impending on his left. As his reserves were already of the smallest, he had to call on his artillery to strengthen this part of the line. The twenty guns of Johnston's division, which had repulsed Mott's attack the day before, were ordered to be withdrawn from the apex of the angle and transferred to the left.

Towards morning, however, Johnston obtained information that the enemy were massing in his front and the guns were ordered back to their original station, but the darkness delayed their progress, so that they were unable to get into action before the assault was delivered.

Meanwhile, the II Corps had moved from its position on the right, and passing in rear of the army had formed under cover of night in two columns at about 1,200 yards from the apex of the angle. Birney's division was on the right with Mott's division in rear. Barlow's division formed the left column and Gibbon's division followed close behind his left.

Owing to the morning being foggy the assault was somewhat delayed, but when it was eventually launched at 4 30 a.m. it came with a velocity and impetus for which Ewell's troops were not prepared. They had barely time to stand to their arms, and failed entirely to check the onslaught.

Capture of the Salient. Birney and Mott's regiments poured over the parapets on the west face of the angle and for 400 yards along the west side of the salient, on the top of the half-roused troops of Dole's brigade. Nearly the whole brigade was captured. Barlow's massed brigades, inclining somewhat to their left, missed the apex and struck the east face of the angle, and Gibbon's division rushing in on Barlow's left immediately afterwards carried the trenches for several hundred yards on the east side of the salient. Johnston's division on Ewell's right was swept away. The general and one of the brigadiers were made prisoners with almost the entire division. The twenty guns which had that moment arrived shared their fate. Two only got into action, the remainder being captured before they could unlimber.

But the rapidity and violence of the assault destroyed all order and formation among the assailants. At the moment when the confusion was greatest the inevitable counter-attack came from the troops who had never once lost a position. More than a third of Ewell's attenuated corps were lost. Only Gordon's division was intact behind his right, with two brigades of Rodes in reserve on his left, but their extraordinary valour equalized everything else. Just as Hancock had sent back word that he "had finished up Johnston and was going into Early," Gordon's incomparable troops charged his disordered masses and hurled them back across the breastworks they had just stormed. At the same time Rodes' two brigades performed the same marvellous feat against the divisions of Birney and Mott.

Recapture of the Salient.

These reserves had constructed a line of works across the gorge of the salient. Hancock's victorious troops coming unexpectedly upon this second line were heavily repulsed from it, and the counter-charge immediately followed.

G.C.

Within an hour the enemy was ejected from the salient, and it seems incredible that this was effected by hardly more than a third of their number.

This assault and its repulse is an excellent illustration of the rule prescribing that assaulting columns must invariably be followed by formed bodies to resist the counter-attack of the enemy's reserves. The II Corps charged in what was really one dense line, with the men crowded together and nothing whatever behind them. They remained thus unsupported for an hour and a half.

But although Ewell's troops had managed to clear the enemy out of their position, they failed to loosen his hold upon the breastworks

Two divisions of the VI Corps (Getty and Ricketts) arrived to reinforce Hancock's right and joined in about the intersection of the west face of the angle with the trenches continuing south-west. This point seems to have been the " Bloody " Angle where thick trees were cut down by the bullets.

All the reinforcements that Lee dared to send to Ewell were three brigades of Early's corps, for Anderson was threatened by the V Corps and Cutler's division of the VI, and the loss of his lines would have involved all the troops in the salient.

Fight at the Angle. Nevertheless Gordon and Rodes, with these three brigades, making in all ten brigades, disputed the parapets of the angle with the six divisions of the II and VI Corps, throughout the day and far into the night.

The two sides manned the same parapet, and there began one of the most ferocious contests in the history of war. Crowding against either side of the barrier the frenzied men shot and stabbed at each other's faces across the crest and into each other's bodies between the logs. Rank after rank pressed eagerly up and fought savagely until they sank down into the ditch to make room for more. The dead lay in places four deep on either side of the breastwork. Guns were brought up to the angles and enfiladed the trenches until they were put out of action. Men leapt upon the parapet and standing fired with rifles handed to them until they were shot down and replaced by others. Some of the logs were entirely disintegrated into splinters by the bullets, and in places the forest was literally shot down, and this continued for hours.

It is one of those instances of the remarkable effect produced on men by certain conditions of battle. These instances show that under certain influences, not only individuals, but masses of ordinary civilized persons will exhibit a complete absence of the sense of fear and will behave in a manner which is actually insane. This form of mania is a product of the primitive aggressive instinct of the stronger animals, and as it is generally found associated with victory, is to be encouraged. Any overdiscipline amounting to individual repression tends to make troops less subject to its occurrence.

Operations of IX and V Corps. On the Federal left the IX Corps had assailed Early's left simultaneously with the main attack. One division (Potter's) gained a temporary lodgment in the works, but was almost immediately driven out. Repeated attacks were made by the three other divisions but they all failed to reach Early's trenches. They established themselves, however, close to the position and erected breastwork there.

Between 9 and 10 a.m. the V Corps and Cutler's division of the VI Corps attacked Anderson's centre in the hope that he would be found to have been weakened in order to reinforce the salient. A vigorous attack was made, but was repulsed with such heavy loss that it soon became apparent that Anderson was in full strength. There being no prospect of success the attack was stopped and Cutler was ordered to reinforce his own corps at the "Bloody" Angle. The V Corps was ordered to follow and assail the same point. The withdrawal and transfer of these troops occupied the whole afternoon, and before they were re-formed for the new attack Grant had determined to abandon his effort against the salient.

The fighting at the angle continued till evening. During the night most of the Federal troops were withdrawn, but at the "Bloody" Angle the fighting continued in a desultory manner till 3 a.m. on the 13th.

Lee withdraws from Salient. Lee now decided that he had not sufficient strength to hold the salient, and before dawn the Confederates also fell back to the work which Gordon's troops had constructed across the gorge of the salient. This line connected Anderson's right with Early's left.

The total Federal losses on May 12 are given at over 6,800. There is the usual uncertainty as to those of Lee which are estimated at between four and five thousand with as many prisoners. But it is difficult to believe that the Confederate losses were the greater, for they repulsed several assaults on the left and right in which the enemy must have suffered far the most severely.

Losses.

From May 4 to 12 Grant had lost about 30,600 men, a sufficient excuse for desisting, for a time at any rate, from further offensive movements, yet so far from being dismayed he issued instruction for an immediate resumption of the attacks.

Although Lee's left and centre had proved impregnable, his right remained to be tried, and on the night of the 13th the right half of the Federal army was transferred to its left to make another general assault on the 14th. This appears to have been more than nature could endure, for the rain descended and poured for a week. This probability of rain following heavy firing in cloudy weather is a factor to be considered in planning movements to take place immediately after a battle.

Failure of Plans for May 14. On the night of the 13th the V Corps set out to march to the left of the XI Corps with orders to assault at 4 a.m. on the 14th. The

VI Corps followed and was to attack simultaneously with the V Corps along the Massaponax Church Road. The instruction to Hancock and Burnside (II and IX Corps) were that they should hold themselves in readiness to attack, but to await actual orders to do so.

But throughout the night torrents of rain fell turning the country roads into quagmires and making the passage of wheels almost impossible. The V Corps did not reach its station until 6 a.m. By that time the ranks were depleted by straggling, and the men so exhausted as to be obviously incapable of effecting anything. The assault, being out of the question, was countermanded.

Later in the day the VI Corps arrived on the left of the V, much in the same condition.

However, in the afternoon, when the troops were somewhat rested, a success was gained on the Massaponax road where the Confederates held a hill in advance of Early's right. This was seized by two brigades of the V Corps who drove back the defenders. Early's men promptly sallied out and retook it, but Warren sent in more troops and eventually recaptured and held the eminence. This was the only fighting on the 14th.

Grant's intentions having become apparent Lee began to make his dispositions to meet them. Anderson's divisions were, in succession, transferred to the right. Mahone's division moved during the 14th, but Field's division did not arrive till midnight, and Kershaw's did not follow till 24 hours later.

It was certainly unfortunate therefore, for the Federals, that Grant's plans for an attack on Lee's right on the morn of the 14th came to nought. These plans would have brought the IX, V, and VI Corps against Early's corps, and would have resulted in a stronger combination than that of the 12th, in which Ewell's corps was assailed by two corps, less one division. On the other hand the Confederates had learned to construct works of great strength, and they repeatedly proved their ability to hold them against vastly superior numbers.

Anderson's corps was eventually disposed on Early's right and extended to Snell's bridge over the Po river.

The 15th, 16th and 17th were spent by both sides in strengthening their works, and the V and VI Corps advanced their parapets some distance nearer the position, and batteries were erected mostly in front of the V Corps.

On the 15th two divisions of the II Corps were withdrawn from the right and placed in rear of the V Corps, so as to be able to act on either flank as required. One division of the II Corps remained on the right of the IX Corps.[1]

Grant's Plan for May 18.
The heavy losses incurred at the salient on the 12th seem to have persuaded Grant that his favourite method of straightforward general attacks was too costly. The surprise at-

[1] On the 13th Mott's division of the II Corps was consolidated with Birney's.

tack designed by the 14th having been foiled by the weather, he did not attempt to pursue the scheme after it had become revealed to the enemy, but resorted to another artifice in hopes of taking Lee off his guard. Trusting that his threat on the right of the position might have induced Lee to weaken his left, (which now consisted of the retrenchment across salient,) he transferred the whole of the VI Corps from his extreme left to his extreme right. The movement was made under cover of the night of the 17th. Before morning on the 18th this corps, with the whole of the II Corps, was deployed opposite the retrenchment to make a surprise attack at daybreak. The IX Corps was to attack on their left and the V Corps was to open with the massed artillery and be ready to advance if ordered.

Ewell's corps, however, was still in their retrenchment, and his men were not to be caught twice. The work was of great strength and the assault was very severely repulsed. As soon as Meade saw that position was fully manned he immediately ordered the cessation of the attack.

Repulse of Assault of May 18.

After this failure Grant decided to abandon his attempts to break through Lee's position at Spottsylvania, and determined to repeat his former tactics of moving towards Richmond.

The VI Corps was returned to its position on the left and the II Corps resumed its post in rear of the centre under orders to cross the Ny River on the night of the 19th and to commence the flank movement on the night of the 20th.

Lee, however, divined his adversary's intention and sought to profit by his extension On the afternoon of the 19th Ewell advanced from his works and, forming across the right of the IX Corps, attacked it with some initial success, driving the enemy back some distance, and capturing some wagons of the trains on the Fredericksburg road in rear. But the II Corps had not started on its march, and a division of reinforcements had that day arrived from Richmond in rear of the IX Corps Two divisions of the II Corps and a division of the V were hurried against Ewell who was repulsed with considerable loss. Early, who was in readiness to take advantage of the success of Ewell's operation, attempted to create a diversion by attacking the VI Corps, but desisted as soon as it appeared that no advantage was to be gained.

<small>Ewell's Sortie.</small>

This was Lee's last offensive movement against Grant. He evidently hoped to find the Federal army extended on its move southwards, and as soon as he observed that this was not the case he immediately relinquished his design.

In conjunction with the assault on the 18th Grant ordered special efforts by the artillery. From works of officers on Grant's personal staff, who closely chronicled every word and action of his, it appears that this was the only occasion in the campaign on which he called upon his guns, and there is no mention of artillery preparation to any of his assaults. In these works artillery is scarcely ever alluded to, and on his advance from Spottsylvania he returned nearly a third of his guns to Washington. This makes it obvious that he had little use for them, and the inference must be that he failed to appreciate their value.

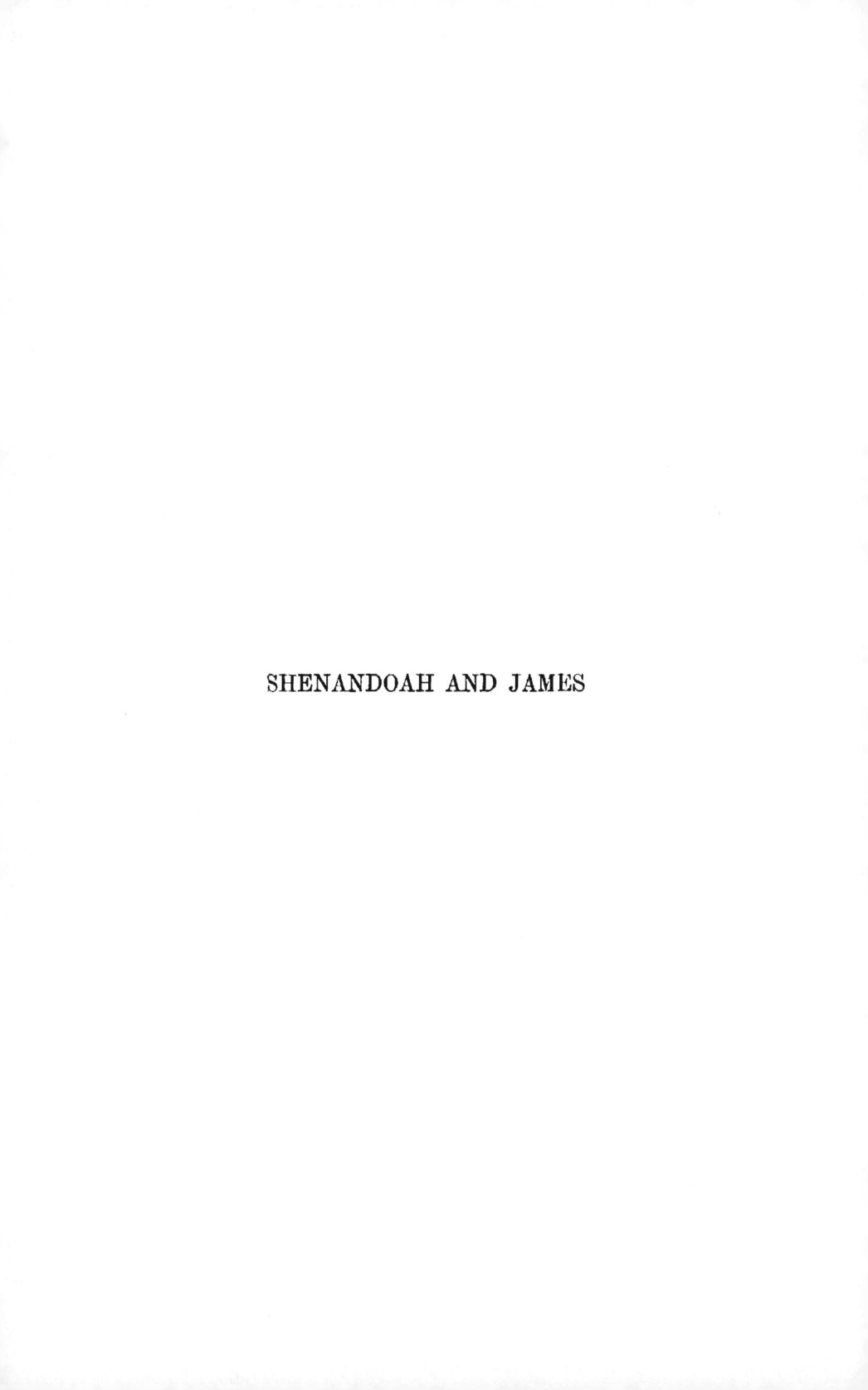

SHENANDOAH AND JAMES

CHAPTER VII

SHENANDOAH AND JAMES

BEFORE following Grant's progress further it will be convenient to note the fortunes of the two subsidiary movements in Virginia, viz. those in the Shenandoah Valley and on the James.

The Valley.
The mountain system of the Alleghannies passes along the Western border of Virginia in a series of parallel ranges. The most easterly range is named the Blue Ridge. Along the northern half of the border the Blue Ridge recedes somewhat from the main system, forming the Shenandoah Valley. This valley is some 120 miles long and the bed about 20 miles across. Its rivers flow into the Potomac at Harper's Ferry, and the direction is NNE. Staunton, at the head of the valley, is about 110 miles almost due west from Richmond.

Protected on the east by the Blue Ridge, which is only passable to troops at the gaps or passes, and secured on the west by the impracticable barrier of the Alleghannies, the valley formed a covered way by which an army could move from Virginia to the Potomac, or vice versa, skirting the main theatre of war and secure from the forces operating there. It was several times used thus by the Confederates with great advantage.

It was also important as a source of supply to Richmond, being an extremely fertile tract.

Virginia Railways
From Staunton the Virginia Central railway ran via Charlottesville and Gordonsville to Richmond. As the line terminated a few miles west of Staunton its utility to the Confederates was only to convey supplies to Richmond or troops to the valley. Thus the occupation of Staunton by the enemy did not effect the military railway system of the Confederacy. Fifty miles south of Staunton, however, there ran a more important line of railway, which, running from Richmond, WSW., connected it with Chattanooga. This was the Tennessee Railway.[1] On Sherman taking Chattanooga this line lost its value as a means of transferring troops to and from Tennessee, but it still formed the main line of supply to Richmond from the south and south-west portions of Virginia. From Lynchburg, due south of Staunton on this line, the Orange and Alexandria railway runs north west through Charlottesville, Gordonsville and Manassas to Washington. The line from Staunton (Virginia Central) joins it at Charlottesville and leaves it at Gordonsville Upon Grant's advance the Alexandria railway became

[1] From Lynchburg to Petersburg it was known as the South Side Ry.

useless north of Gordonsville, and the Virginian Central railway was constantly threatened, for Grant's first intention was to advance southwards across this latter line. If he had gained it on the North Anna, as he expected, and tried to do, the supplies from the valley and the western portion of the State would have had to be brought round by Lynchburg. Thus the importance of Lynchburg becomes manifest.

Grant counted on cutting the Virginian Central north of Richmond; therefore if he could also seize Lynchburg the whole of the west side and the south-west corner of the State would be cut off from the capital.

Objective of Crook and Sigel.

This was what he hoped the columns of Crook and Sigel on his right might be able to effect. As an invasion in co-operation with the main body the scheme had no merit, and it is evident that Grant did not expect to derive any strategical or tactical advantage from it. But as an expedition to cut off supplies from Richmond and curtail the resources of the main army it has some excuse. Whether this excuse amounts to a justification of the expedition is the subject investigated in this chapter.

Grant's plan for the spring of 1864 ordered an advance of the Federal force in West Virginia to destroy the Tennessee railway, and at the same time another advance was to be made down the Shenandoah Valley. The forces were then to unite at Staunton and move via

Charlottesville on Lynchburg. The Tennessee line crosses the watershed of the Alleghannies some 40 miles west of Lynchburg, and enters the valleys which give rise to the Kanawha river, a tributary of the Ohio The upper basin of the river is a mountainous district formed by the western features of the main system. These higher valleys were held by small Confederate orces covering the line, and the Federal force in West Virginia, consisting of some 6,000 infantry under Crook and 2,000 cavalry under Averil, were lower down the river at the foot of the mountains. The shortest route by which Crook could carry out his orders to destroy the line brought him on to it at Newbern, west of the Alleghanies. Starting on May 3, he defeated the Confederate detachments on May 9 in the mountains north of the line and reached Newbern, where he burned the railway bridge across the Kanawha River. Averil with the cavalry had at the same time tried to reach the railway further west at Wytheville and Saltville, but had been repulsed Both forces withdrew immediately to Meadow Bluff They had not effected much, for they had only isolated the extreme S.W. corner of Virginia, and the small traffic from that portion was easily transportable by road to above Newbern ; for it will be remembered the line further west to Knoxville and Chattanooga was already in the hands of Sherman. However, they had carried out the first part of their orders and were pre-

Crook's Advance and Repulse.

paring to move on Staunton when the plan was upset by the defeat of the valley column.

This force, started from Winchester on April 30, and consisted of about 6,500 men under Sigel. Sigel, very reasonably, objected to marching unsupported with so small a force up a valley which had ever proved so fortunate to the Confederates.[1] He held that his left was open to attack through any of the gaps in the Blue Ridge, and that in any case Crook should move simultaneously on Staunton. Grant seems to have concurred in his argument and sent word about May 10 that he did not require him to go beyond Strasburg, evidently intending that a further advance should be postponed till Crook had returned from his raid and could participate.

Sigel's Advance and Repulse.

Sigel, however, got information that Breckenridge, who was defending the valley, had only 3,000 men with him and determined to advance. On May 15 he met the Federal force which was coming to meet him near Newmarket. It turned out to be equal to his own and, being better handled, defeated him with a loss of 800 men and five guns. Sigel then fell back to Strasburg, where he was removed from command and replaced by Hunter. Hunter was reinforced from Washington by 2,500 men and some guns about the 20th.

The news of Sigel's defeat was very welcome to Lee,

---

[1] Ord, who was originally ordered by Grant to carry out the movement under Sigel, disliked it so that he asked to be relieved.

who at that time was very hard pressed at Spottsylvania, and he sent Breckenridge orders to join the army of Virginia with nearly the whole of his force.

This demonstrates the facility with which convergent attacks can be dealt with by a force on interior lines, and is another argument against the valley expedition.

Breckenridge's victory stayed Crook's advance automatically, and enabled Lee to leave the valley practically ungarrisoned till June In his defence of the North Anna River, May 20-28, and at the desperate fighting at Cold Harbour, June 2-3, he was able to use almost the whole of that force which the valley column was intended to keep occupied. Therefore it is seen that Sigel's advance, so far from aiding Grant's movement in any way, deprived him of force throughout his advance to Richmond. It is true that the amount of this force was comparatively small, and the valley movement did deprive Lee of Breckenridge's troops during the fighting in the Wilderness and at Spottsylvania, but the argument is not thereby affected materially.

Sigel was undoubtedly right in his opinion that Crook and Averil should have accompanied him in his advance. Had they done so Breckenridge would have been greatly outnumbered, especially in cavalry, and could hardly have escaped defeat. During the month of May Lee could have spared no reinforcements, and Crook and Sigel's force of 12,000 ought to have reached Charlottesville, while Averil with the 2,000 cavalry might have reached Lynchburg.

But even if we suppose that such a success had been gained by the proper co-operation of Crook and Sigel, and Lynchburg seized, it could not have been of any permanent or real value so long as Lee could retain the interior lines, i e., as long as he could keep Grant on the outside of the semicircle formed by Charlottesville, the North Anna and Richmond. If he could continue to hold him there, it was certain that eventually an opportunity would occur of detaching troops to Charlottesville, for Grant could not continue to attack unsuccessfully for an indefinite period.

If on the other hand Grant could have broken through the semicircle, the interior line to Charlottesville would have become his, and any force there or in the valley would have had to fall back or risk being cut off. Therefore, we see that the best chance of securing the valley lay, not in a subsidiary operation, but with the main army of the Potomac. Lee once driven into the semicircle, operations from Charlottesville based on the Orange railway could have been commenced against Lynchburg with a good chance of success.

There is evidence, however, that Grant hoped, and indeed expected, to drive Lee due south across the North Anna, for in the orders to Butler on the James he indicates a junction with him west of Richmond. Had his hopes been realized all would have been well with the valley expedition (had it been properly combined with Crook's force).

In this light criticism of the valley movement may be modified to the extent that it should have been postponed until Grant had broken through the circumference of Lee's interior lines.

Otherwise it deserves nothing but condemnation. Its influence on the main operations was to slightly weaken both forces—Grant's throughout the campaign and Lee's for the first half of May. Its defeat had a favourable influence on the spirit of the Confederates.

Hunter's Advance to Staunton. On June 2 a second advance was made up the valley by the reinforced army of Hunter; but the strategical situation had now completely changed, for Grant had been repulsed from the North Anna and compelled to move eastwards. Lee had retained his interior lines and the army of the Potomac was before Cold Harbour, north-east of Richmond. Not only was co-operation between that army and Hunter's force impossible, but the former was now no longer in a position to exercise any influence on the situation in the valley, except by keeping the whole of Lee's force engaged.

The arguments against this second advance are the same as against the first, with the added objection that its hope of permanent success was diminished by the location of the Potomac army, and by the fact that the strength of the Richmond defences increased Lee's facility for acting against subsidiary movements.

On June 2 Hunter with 8,500 advanced to Staunton.

The valley had been nearly denuded of troops, and the garrison of Lynchburg was hurriedly brought up to defend it. The Confederates, under W. F. Jones, about 5,000, attempted to stay the advance at Piedmont, a few miles in front of Staunton, but were routed on June 5, with a loss of some 2,000 and their commander, who was killed. The remainder fell back to Waynesboro, covering the Rockfish Gap the pass by which the railway crosses the Blue Ridge to Charlottesville. Hunter reached Staunton on the 6th, where he was joined by Crook and Averil. This reinforcement brought his force up to 17,000 and 33 guns, and on June 10 he proceeded to move on Lynchburg.

Grant's Measures for Co-operation. On June 3 Grant had been repulsed from Cold Harbour in such a manner as to convince him that the positions were only to be taken by regular siege works. He ordered a cessation of the attacks and stated that his object was now to retain the army of Virginia in its position until Hunter was well on the way to Lynchburg, and that this purpose were more easily effected by keeping Lee out of Richmond defences than by driving him into them. The army was idle for nine days.

The process of reasoning by which this order was evolved is not clear. Lee had just conclusively proved that Grant had not the power to drive him into the Richmond defences, and Grant by his actions then and subsequently admitted this. So his statement that he refrained from further attacks on Cold Harbour because he was afraid of driving Lee back into Richmond is not very acceptable. Further, his object being to prevent reinforcement of the valley between the 4th and 10th, was futile to argue that inaction was a necessary condition, for it can be reduced to an absurdity by saying that further offensive movements might have induced Lee to voluntarily weaken his force. The presence of Grant's force was enough to deter Lee from detaching any considerable force, and demonstrations might have retained his whole army in position, but the complete inaction that ensued after June 3 enabled him to send Breckenridge's 3,000 men back to cover Charlottesville on June 7, after learning of Jones' defeat.

The only support extended to Hunter was two divisions of cavalry dispatched under Sheridan to cut the Virginia Central Railway between Louisa Court House and Gordonsville. The Confederate cavalry under Hampton and FitzHugh Lee started on the 8th to defend it. The forces met at Trevylian Station on the 11th, and although the Confederates had rather the worst of the first encounter, Sheridan found himself unable to effectually damage the line in their presence, and hearing that Hunter was not moving to Charlottesville to meet him he retired on the night of the 12th. In this action both sides claimed the victory.

Trevylian Station.

From June 4 to 11 the Potomac army lay idle. On

the 12th it was withdrawn from its position before Cold Harbour and marched to the James to operate against the Petersburg defences. On the 11th Hunter reached Lexington on his road to Lynchburg, and on the 13th Early's Corps proceeded from the army of Virginia to reinforce Lynchburg. In the face of these dates Grant's order of the 3rd can only be regarded as a hurriedly prepared excuse to the army for discontinuing the offensive at Cold Harbour, and it must be assumed that the solicitude expressed for Hunter's expedition did not really represent Grant's attitude towards it. This is the only possible conclusion, for as soon as Hunter had left Staunton on June 11 to complete the most important part of his mission, Grant withdrew from Lee's front (June 12) and moving to the south of Richmond drew Lee into its defences, thus bringing about the very culmination which he had expressed himself anxious to avoid, and thereby liberating Early on June 13 to proceed to Lynchburg.

Hunter's Advance on Lynchburg. Hunter was joined by Crook and Averil at Staunton on the 10th, and with this combined force of 17,000 marched on the 11th to Lexington across the watershed between the sources of the Shenandoah and James Rivers. At the same time he despatched a division of cavalry to break the railway between Charlottesville and Lynchburg. Grant's intention was that he should have gone via Charlottesville, but Hunter thought that the forcing of Rockfish Gap would cause delay, and held that his quickest and best route was the direct line across the hills. At Lexington he remained during the 12th and 13th waiting for the cavalry division to rejoin him, and then proceeded. On the 17th, his advance guards were met by the troops of Breckenridge five miles outside Lynchburg.

Breckenridge had moved by rail to Charlottesville on the 9th, and being joined by the remnants of Jones' army from Waynesborough proceeded at once to Lynchburg.

Early left Richmond on the 13th, and took the same route, joining Breckenridge on the 17th (the damage done to the line by the cavalry having been repaired).

Hunter attacked Lynchburg on the 18th, and although the fighting was indecisive, it became apparent to him that he had no prospect of success. As he was running short of supplies and ammunition, and was out of reach of any base, he commenced his retreat on the same night. But his position now had become a difficult one, for if he retreated the way he had come, Early, moving by rail to Charlottesville, would intercept him at Staunton. So he was compelled to fall back westwards into the Kanawha Valley, thereby yielding the entire Shenandoah Valley to the Confederates.

<small>Hunter's Repulse and Flight.</small>

Hunter has been adversely criticized for not following Grant's instruction to advance via Charlottesville, but it is not easy to see that he would have bettered the situation. Had he reached Charlottesville on the 12th and proceeded to Lynchburg he would have been caught between Early and Breckenridge. His force was quite incapable of holding Charlottesville and capturing Lynchburg as well, and his mission was essentially against the latter place. So it would seem that he did better in advancing by the least exposed route which offered some chance of escape. The adverse criticism therefore is wrongly laid on Hunter, whose only misfortune was in having to carry out the scheme, and the blame lies on the authority, which, having commanded it, neglected to take measures to support it.

In any case the scheme was of very doubtful merit, even while pressure could be applied on Lee; but to remove that pressure in the middle of the operation was simply to make positively certain of its failure, and this is what Grant effected by his withdrawal from Cold Harbour on June 12.

Early pursued the defeated columns westwards until the 22nd and then returned. Hunter by forced and painful marches reached Gauley bridge on the Kanawha on the 27th. His troops were then so broken down by fatigue and starvation that they could not be made available for the defence of Washington in July.

The defeat of this misbegotten movement, however, was only a small part of the penalties with which the Federals had to pay for it.

As early as June 13, when the force was despatched to crush Hunter, Lee had seen the possibilities opened by his adversaries' mistake, and he then authorized Early to use his discretion in making a counter-stroke on Washington via the undefended Shenandoah Valley.

Early's Raid on Washington.

Early returning from the pursuit of Hunter reached Staunton on June 27, and resolved to follow Lee's suggestion. He advanced up the valley, reaching Winchester on July 2, and, although he now passes out of the limits of this work, it is necessary to follow him in order to fully appreciate the baleful influences of Grant's valley movement. On Early's approach with some 17,000 men, Sigel with a small force at Martinsburg retired across the Potomac and held the Maryland Heights, commanding Harper's Ferry. Early therefore had to cross at Shepherdstown, and on his way to Frederick he delayed a day to make an attack on Sigel's position. It proved unsuccessful, and Early pushed on, reaching Frederick at dawn on July 9. Three miles beyond Frederick some 5,000 Federals stood to oppose him. These represented more than a third of the total force available for the defences of Washington.

They were powerless to stay the Confederate advance, and on the 9th were swept out of its path with a loss of 2,000. The road to Washington now lay open, and by 6 p.m. on the 11th Early's divisions were deployed against the works of the capital, but the troops were too weary to attack that day. Only on that same afternoon the VI Corps, which had been hurriedly brought from Petersburg by sea, arrived in Washington. Their arrival became known to Early, and wisely concluding that his chance had passed, he retreated the way he had come.

Had Early not delayed at the Maryland Heights, or had he gained a day elsewhere, or had the VI Corps lost a day, any of these contingencies might have brought about the capture of Washington which, even if the possession had been only temporary, would have been disastrous to the Union cause.

It now becomes apparent how grave and how far-reaching may be the effects of even a small strategical error.

Grant's subsidiary movement by the valley achieved nothing, and by uncovering the approach to Washington it nearly cost the Federals the loss of their capital. In addition to this, it caused the suspension of the July operations against Petersburg for several weeks.

The Operations on the James.

Simultaneously with the valley movement the second subsidiary operation was taking place on the James River.

The army of the James under Butler was about 35,000

strong, in two corps, under W. F. Smith and Gillmore. It was first conveyed to the York River and assembled at the end of April on the south shore of that estuary in order to give the impression that the advance was to be made up the peninsula between that river and the James estuary on the route of the great invasion under McClellan in '62.

On the night of May 4, when the concentration was complete, the troops were re-embarked and conveyed up the estuary of the James to Bermudah Hundred, a small peninsula at the head of the estuary in the confluence of the James and Appomatox rivers. They were disembarked on the 6th and advancing some five miles constructed a line of works across the peninsula at a point where it narrowed to a breadth of about three miles. Just behind the left of this line was a spot known as Point of Rocks, which afforded facilities for bridging the Appomatox River. From this spot the eastern defences of Petersburg were five miles distant. By the roads north of the Appomatox, via Port Walthall Junction, the town was about nine miles distant from the Federal position. The Southern works of Richmond lay about fourteen miles in the opposite direction, and half-way towards them the defenders had a strong, semi-permanent work at Drewry's Bluff on the south bank of the River James, and from it field works ran westwards across the railway and the turnpike road. The main position stretched about $2\frac{1}{2}$ miles westwards from the Bluff, and an advanced line of trenches lay about a mile in front, with its right on a small hill.

Grant's Orders to Butler. Grant's orders to Butler were to march on Richmond, keeping close to the James, and to invest the city on the south. He was further commanded to establish his left on the river above Richmond where, if possible, the army of the Potomac would join him. Butler has been blamed for the failure of this expedition, as being an abnormally inefficient leader and without military training, but a better man might well have been at a loss to carry out such instructions.

On his right lay Richmond, strongly fortified, and for all Butler knew sufficiently strongly held. On his left the stronghold of Petersburg was connected by four lines of railway with the rest of the Confederacy, and formed a rendezvous for the reinforcements from the south to be assembled against him.

His orders demanded not merely that he should place his army on the Petersburg Richmond Railway between these two strong places, but that he should thrust himself through to the east of Richmond, with " his left on the river above the city." In the face of the heavy guns on the north bank it was impossible to use the river as a line of supply, and his communications with Bermudah Hundred would have required half his force to hold them.

Conceivably, Richmond might have fallen to a sudden " coup de main," but the works were very strong and the

James River was not to be crossed in a moment. In the light of subsequent events it is more probable that had Butler, immediately on landing, pushed on to the east of Richmond he would have lost his army. It is quite clear that Grant, in his desire to cut the communication of Richmond with the South, mistook the situation and failed to appreciate at that time that the possession of Petersburg was necessary to that end.

However, his orders were explicit, and it is not surprising to see an inexperienced general under the circumstances behaving with irresolution.

Butler's First Moves. On May 7, Butler sent five brigades to destroy the Richmond-Petersburg railway, but after severe fighting these were driven back by the reinforcements which had already reached Petersburg from the South.

On May 1 the garrisons of Petersburg and Richmond only numbered some 7,000, but most of Pickett's division (of Hill's corps) were close at hand watching Suffolk. The embarkation and destination of Butler's army was ascertained early, and on the 5th all available troops were summoned to Petersburg from the south. Beauregard was brought from South Carolina and placed in command of the force, which finally totalled about 19,000. They were stationed mostly in the Drewry Bluff works.

On the 9th Butler moved out with most of his force, and driving back the force defending the railway, destroyed the line from Chester Station to Swift Creek.

This stream was only three miles from Petersburg, but it was strongly held by Beauregard's rapidly arriving forces, and on the 10th Butler returned to Bermudah Hundred.

On this day he was strongly urged by Smith and Gillmore to cross at Point of Rocks to the south bank of the Appomatox and make an attempt on Petersburg.

This would indeed have been a wise course if it had been pursued three days earlier, for Petersburg might then have been seized and held with inestimable advantage to the Federal cause. But the orders explicitly defined a move on Richmond "keeping close to the James." If Butler had ignored Grant's orders and in defiance of them moved on Petersburg and taken it, his action would have been equivalent to that of Nelson at Copenhagen, and he would have deserved fame. But the character of the whole operation would then have been changed, and we would be dealing with Butler's brilliant raid on Petersburg instead of with Grant's ill-considered movement against Richmond.

Butler cannot be blamed for not possessing a military genius higher than that of his chief, but his movements hereafter were undoubtedly slow and dilatory.

On May 12 he moved out along the Richmond turnpike against Drewry Bluff, and disposed his troops before the position.

Attack on Drewry Bluff. This position consisted of the semi-permanent work round the Bluff mounting heavy guns, and a line of trenches stretching about 2½ miles from the Bluff across the road and railway. About a mile in advance of this main position lay an outer line of trenches connected with it on the left and resting on a small hill on the right.

On May 13, the Federals attacked and Gillmore's corps, turning the right of the outer works, captured this hill. On the 14th, the fighting was resumed and the whole of the outer line carried. An attack on the main position was to have been made on the morning of the 15th, but was abandoned, "owing to lack of troops to make up the assaulting column."

Beauregard's force in the Drewry Bluff position now amounted to three divisions and two cavalry regiments, in all, some 17,000; while Petersburg was held by Whiting with two brigades of infantry and one of cavalry.

Any chance that ever existed of seizing either Richmond or Petersburg had now passed, and on the 16th, Beauregard assumed the offensive. Early in the morning he attacked the enemies' right with one Division, while the other two moved against the trenches which had been lost on the 13th.

The Federal right terminated about one mile from the river, and Beauregard hoped by turning this flank to interpose between Butler and his base at Bermudah Hundred. This he succeeded in doing, but a heavy fog from the river interfered with the manoeuvre and necessitated the withdrawal and realignment of his left division. The attacks of his other two divisions on the rest of the position were repulsed and Whiting, who had advanced from Petersburg to attack the Federals' rear, was held in check by a division at Walthall Junction.

Blockade of Butler's Army. But the threat on his right was sufficient to afford Butler an excuse to retire, and he thereupon committed a blunder for which he alone is responsible. During the night he withdrew to his original position in Bermudah Hundred and allowed Beauregard to construct a line of works close in front of him, which blockaded him in the peninsula.

The fighting had been heavy and the Federals had suffered the more severely, losing 3,500 against 2,000 of their adversaries; but there is no excuse for Butler's precipitate retreat before an army of half his strength.

No doubt the impracticable orders under which he laboured engendered a feeling of insecurity in his mind, and the evident hopelessness of his task could not have tended to inspire him. But he might at least have made an effort to maintain himself in a position to command the Petersburg Richmond Railway. It seems that he passively submitted to being imprisoned, and did not even attempt to interfere with the constructing of the barrier which shut him in.

Grant, on hearing of his incarceration, ordered him on the 22nd to send half his army, under Smith, by sea, to White House to join the Potomac army. The remainder were to hold the James estuary up to City Point and later, when the whole of the Potomac army was transferred to the south of Petersburg, the remainder of Butler's force was also withdrawn and joined the main force.

Smith's corps did not arrive at White House till May 30, but Beauregard, the moment he had entrapped Butler, despatched a division to Lee, and soon after followed it with another.[1]

The reports of Sigel's defeat on May 15, and Butler's on May 16, reached Grant simultaneously on the 17th, just after the failure of his last assault on Lee's position at Spottsylvania, and his first comments were to the effect that Lee would at once reinforce himself from Richmond, the valley, and the head of the Kanawha.

The influence of these two subsidiary movements may now be summarized.

Crook destroyed a railway bridge in an immaterial locality, and while he was so engaged his co-operator, Sigel, suffered a defeat whereby a Confederate force was liberated to join its main army. Butler caused the withdrawal of several garrisons and detachments from the Southern States, and his defeat also liberated two divisions to assist Lee at the North Anna and at Cold Harbour.

Hunter's advance was really a third subsidiary movement and its disastrous effect has already been commented on.

[1] Pickett's Division reach Lee at North Anna on the 23rd, and Hoke's Division arrived at Totopotomoy on the 30th May

Calculating Butler's force at 33,000, and Crook and Sigel at 18,000, and allowing 8,000 to defend the lower end of the valley, it may be said that during the whole of May Grant was deprived of some 43,000 men in his operations against Lee. Counting Pickett's division at 5,000, and the troops in the valley and West Virginia at 1,300, Lee was deprived during the same period of 18,000, of which some 8,000 of Breckenridge's troops were available part of the time.

NORTH ANNA

CHAPTER VIII

NORTH ANNA

THE repulse of the attack on the retrenchment at Spottsylvania on May 18 finally persuaded Grant against renewing his assaults on Lee's works, and he determined to continue his move to the left. On the 19th the II Corps returned to the left of the line to commence the movement next day; but on the afternoon of the 19th Ewell attacked the Federal right, necessitating the hurried recall of the II Corps to reinforce that flank.

Ewell being repulsed, the move to the left was continued; but with an added design. Grant's despatches at this period show that he was beginning to doubt his ability to prevail against entrenchments held by such a master of defence as Lee, and he expresses in these a fervent desire to bring about an action in the open field.

Grant's Plans on May 20. Ewell's attack on his right suggested to him a scheme by which he might induce the much desired condition. That attack was represented in the Confederate despatches as a reconnaissance, but there is evidence (Early's Memoirs) to show that Lee intended to follow up any marked success with a general offensive movement. This was also Grant's conception of it, and he resolved to tempt Lee to repeat the operation. His design to encompass this end was to send the II Corps round the Confederate right, a day's march or more in advance of the army, in the hope that by drawing an attack upon itself it might be instrumental in bringing on a general engagement under circumstances which would not afford Lee an opportunity of entrenching.

The II Corps returned to its post on the Federal left on the morning of the 20th, and at 11 p.m. the same evening started for Guinea Station, eight miles distant *en route* for Milford Station via the left bank of the Mattapony River.

The remaining corps faced the enemy's position; the IX Corps on the right, the V Corps in the centre and the VI Corps on the left.

Under Grant's original plan Hancock was to bring on an engagement by crossing the Mattapony at Milford and inviting attack there, upon Lee moving in that direction the V Corps followed by the IX Corps were to move due south via the Telegraph Road and fall on the enemy's left, while the VI Corps followed the route of the II Corps to assist it.

Guinea Station was held by the Confederate flank guards, and Hancock's arrival there being immediately reported, Lee, on the night of the 20th, brought Ewell from his left and extended his corps along the Po, covering the crossing of the Telegraph road at Stannard's Mills.

Alteration of Grant's Plans. His appearance there on the morning of the 21st caused Grant to make a modification of his plan which amounted to its abandonment. Instead of keeping quiet and leaving his decoy to do its work he began to move towards it. Throughout the night of the 20th and morning of the 21st Hancock was pushing on rapidly via Bowling Green to Milford, and during the afternoon he crossed the river there. His passage was disputed by a brigade of reinforcements from Richmond which were *en route* to join Lee, but they were easily driven off with some loss and Hancock established himself on the south bank Grant, fearing for his safety, started the V Corps to follow him at 10 a.m. on the 21st. This movement, added to the reports of Hancock's advance down the Mattapony, convinced Lee that a movement was in progress round his right towards Richmond, and he promptly fell back to oppose it. On the 21st Ewell's and Anderson's corps started for Hanover junction by the Telegraph Road, while Hill, who had resumed command of his own corps from Early, remained in position till late that night.

This put an end to the scheme for bringing Lee to battle in the open. If Grant had remained quiescent on the 21st Lee would probably have also held his ground, and on the 22nd Hancock's corps by advancing towards the Telegraph Road could scarcely have failed to bring on an engagement. It is true that Lee would probably have fallen on with two of his corps and might have severely handed the II Corps but Grant's original plan not only accepted that risk but was designed to bring about that event. At the same time Lee would have been obliged to leave at least one corps to hold back the three corps on the Po river, so Grant had an equally good or better chance of overwhelming a Confederate corps in his turn and should have reached Hancock in time to save him. In which case the 2nd Manassas might have been repeated in favour of the Federals. Grant and Hancock, however, were not Lee and Jackson, so the plan was abandoned for safer methods.

The V Corps proceeded to Guinea Station on the morning of the 21st and lay there that night while the IX and VI Corps retained their positions.

Lee's Situation. On that night the Federal army was considerably separated, and certain writers have accused Lee of want of enterprise in not taking advantage of this separation. The briefest consideration of Lee's situation is sufficient to dispose of these criticisms. The three corps of Grant's army which lay behind the Po river greatly exceeded Lee's strength. The two corps on the right were strongly entrenched. The V corps was only eight miles distant, within easy reach of the others, and all three were covering the line

NORTH ANNA

to their base at Fredricksburg. So there was small hope of success in attacking any of these. In order to attack Hancock's corps Lee would have had to retain these three corps with sufficient force to prevent them from falling on his left rear while he reached the Mattapony at Milford. The V Corps at Guinea Station was several miles nearer to Hancock than was Lee's centre, and it was obviously moving to join him. Moreover Hancock could at any time retire behind the Mattapony river, and if necessary fall back towards a base at Port Royal on the Rappahannock estuary. It is not surprising, therefore, that Lee himself saw no opportunity of taking the offensive.

The device of detaching the II Corps as a bait might conceivably have succeeded had it been more conspicuously and longer displayed, but movement of the V Corps was sufficient to deter Lee from doing anything so unwise as to play Grant's game in risking a battle in the open against a greatly superior force.

On hearing of the movement of the II Corps towards Milford and seeing the V Corps moving in the same direction he concluded that Grant was making a wide movement along the left bank of the Mattapony to seize a crossing over the Pamunkey river and hurried back to intercept him.

Change of Tactics. It should also be remarked here that while Grant had been compelled to modify his tactics of "hammering" in favour of manoeuvring, Lee's attitude towards his opponents had also undergone a change with the advent of Grant. Hitherto Lee had had to deal with commanders of inferior military capacity. In other words with an inferior army, for the incapacity of a chief eventually infects all the ranks of his command. On Grant's assumption of command the influence of his capacity is at once seen in the actions of his generals and troops. The indecision and apprehensive hesitation which had hitherto marked the progress of the Potomac army immediately became determined action and steadfast valour. The fighting in the Wilderness region brought home to Lee that the Federal divisions were now no longer to be driven like sheep before brigades, and that in fact the northern soldiers individually were becoming a match for his own veterans.

Excepting Ewell's tentative operation of May 19, the Battle of the Wilderness was the last positive offensive action by the army of Virginia in the field. Thereafter never once did Lee dare to attempt the brilliant counter-strokes which had so often wrested the victory from overwhelming numbers. In this, only a few of his detractors have seen evidence of failing courage. Actually it is only another exhibition of his genius which enabled him to see that the day for those tactics was passed. His unerring perception told him that his only chance lay in wearing out his enemy, and he would not be tempted to play a false move.

Federal Moves, May 21, 22. On the night of the 21st, however, there was great apprehension in the Federal army for the safety of the II Corps, which led to a further modification of the original plan. The V Corps, which under the first modification was to follow the route of the II, was ordered on the morning of the 22nd to cross the river near Guinea Station and move southwards so as to be nearer Hancock's right. The IX Corps, starting at 3 a.m. on the 22nd, was to try the passage at Stannard's Mills, and if resisted to follow the V Corps. The VI Corps was to follow the IX.

It will be noticed that Grant could not bring himself to carry out his scheme of exposing for long the II Corps to the mercy of Lee. This Corps only reached its position west of Milford on the afternoon of the 21st, and early on the 22nd Grant was hurrying the rest of the army to support it.

On the night of the 21st Grant's headquarters were some miles in advance of the V Corps on the road to Milford, and the Confederate cavalry were at large between him and the II Corps. Some of Hancock's messengers were intercepted, and a brigade had to be ordered up from the V Corps to guard the general's camp. On the same night Lee advanced a small reconnaissance on his left against the works in front of Spottsylvania, which was repulsed by a division of the VI Corps.

At 3 a m. on the 22nd the IX Corps, followed by the VI Corps having found the passage at Stannard's Mills obstructed, moved to Guinea Station, and passing through it early the same morning followed the V Corps southwards. The V Corps moved to Harris Store and the IX to New Bethel. The II Corps which had been incessantly on the move since the 17th was ordered to stand fast while the others came into line.

Lee's Movements, May 21, 22. Meanwhile the army of Virginia was well on its way to Hanover Junction. In the afternoon of the 21st Ewell and Anderson started along the Telegraph Road and reached the Junction on the morning and afternoon of the 22nd. Therefore it appears that the force which held Stannard's Mills and caused the IX and VI Corps to make the long detour via Guinea Station was only a rear guard. Hill, who had now resumed the command of his own corps from Early, started in good time on the 22nd, and having farther to come than the others, his rear guards came in contact with advance guards of the V Corps west of the Telegraph Road on the 22nd (afternoon), and a sharp skirmish ensued. He reached Hanover Junction on the early morning of the 23rd

It now became apparent that if any chance was lost during these manoeuvres it was by the Federal army. If the original scheme had been vigorously pursued and the IX and VI Corps had made a determined effort at Stannard's Mills they might have pushed aside Anderson's rearguards on the night of the 21st and would probably have intercepted Hill's corps, which was twelve hours behind the rest of the Federal army. A general engagement might have resulted. As it was the V Corps on the 22nd came within sight of Hill's trains and captured a number of stragglers.

The criticism of Grant's movement after the Wilderness battle submitted in Chapter IV is also applicable here. The nearer he moved to Richmond the less became his chance of destroying the army of Virginia in the field. The II Corps could certainly have crossed the river at Guinea Station, and might even have surprised the crossing at Stannard's Mills and the attacks might have been continued on the left of the position towards Snell's Bridge with certainly not worse fortune than befel those at North Anna and Cold Harbour. A defeat at Spottsylvania, or in the Wilderness region, would have been far worse for Lee than a defeat on the North Anna and the promptitude of Lee's withdrawal from the Po river is sufficient testimony of his fear of being intercepted there. Had Grant fought to a finish north of the Po, Lee must have eventually given way before his superior and constantly reinforced strength. The Federals would then have been pressing a beaten enemy to their capital instead of manoeuvring an undefeated army round it. The truth seems to be that the attraction of Richmond, aided by the vigour of Lee's resistance, persuaded Grant to depart from his fighting principles and to manoeuvre fruitlessly until he reached a "ne plus ultra" at Cold Harbour.

<small>Reinforcements.</small> At Hanover Junction Lee received his first reinforcements, which had become available consequent on the failure of Butler's enterprise and on Sigel's defeat. Breckenridge came in from the valley with two brigades. Pickett's Division from Beauregard's command came in from Richmond and joined Hill's corps, to which it belonged. These reinforcements are given at about 9,000 by Confederate authorities.

On the 17th Tyler had reached Grant with 8,000, but at the same time a number of regiments were mustered out, leaving his strength about the same as before.

<small>Position on North Anna.</small> Hanover Junction was the intersection of the Fredericksburg Railway with the Virginia Central Railway, and was situated about two miles south of the North Anna River. About half a mile west of the Fredericksburg railway bridge the Telegraph Road crossed the river by a wooden bridge. Above the bridge two fords were known to the Federals—one, Ox Ford, three miles up, and the second, Jericho Ford, six miles up. A third ford at Quarles Mill, between Ox Ford and Jericho, was not shown on the maps and was not discovered till the 24th.

Lee's position was admirably chosen and had the shape of a V, the apex of which rested on the river at Ox Ford, and was flattened, making a face of three-quarters of a mile opposite the ford. The left face ran S.W. for one and a half miles to the Little River. This was held by Hill's corps. The right face lay nearly south-east covering the Junction and terminating in an impassable swamp which extended to the river. It was about two miles long, and with the face of the apex was held by Ewell and Anderson.

Federal Advance, May 23. At 5 a.m. on the 23rd the army of the Potomac advanced from Harris Store, New Bethel and Milford towards Hanover Junction. The II Corps advanced by the Telegraph Road. The V Corps took a road west of the Telegraph Road leading to Jericho Ford and the VI Corps followed it. The IX Corps moved by plantation roads between the II and V Corps.

The II Corps approached the river about noon and came upon some small works on the north bank defending the Telegraph Road bridge. These were vigorously attacked by Birney's division supported by artillery and were immediately carried with considerable loss to the defenders, who were driven precipitately across the bridge. Other works were then observed on the south bank close to the bridge head, and as it was then growing late the passage of the river at this point was not attempted that night.

K

On the Federal right the V Corps reached Jericho Mills also about noon. The river here was 150 feet wide with high banks and the ford breast deep. A small force was immediately pushed across and drove off a regiment which was watching the ford. A pontoon was then laid for the artillery, and by 5 p.m. the whole corps had passed to the south bank. No attempts whatever were made to interfere with the passage, and the V corps was deployed with Crawford's division on the left, Griffin's in the centre and Cutler's on the right. The first two entrenched themselves, but before Cutler could reach his position he was attacked by Wilcox's division of Hill's corps, at 6 p.m. Wilcox gained some initial success, for a brigade of Cutler's was broken and Griffin's right was for some time in danger. But the assailants were eventually repulsed with the loss of some two hundred prisoners.

Passage of River by V Corps, May 23.

Meanwhile the IX Corps, using bad and devious paths, was much delayed and did not arrive at Ox Ford till sunset, when it was too late to attempt a passage. The VI Corps also reached the ford at Jericho late and bivouacked on the north bank. So that on the night of the 23rd only the V Corps was south of the river.

Here undoubtedly an opportunity was lost to the Confederates, but it seems that the presence of the V Corps on the south bank was not known to Lee till the following morning, when he visited the left of the position. He then censured Hill for having allowed the enemy to cross, asking him why he had not driven them back " as General Jackson would have done!" (WHITE.)

Passage of II Corps and Repulse of IX Corps, May 24. Early on the 24th Hancock, finding that the force covering the bridge had been withdrawn during the night, crossed with the whole of his corps.

One division (Potter's) of the IX Corps was transferred to the II Corps and Burnside was ordered to force a passage at Ox Ford with the other two divisions. This proved wholly impracticable in the face of the artillery at the flattened apex of the position. Whereupon Warren was ordered to send his left division, (Crawford's), down the south bank to endeavour to uncover the ford, and a brigade from the II Corps moved up the river with the same object and with orders to connect with Crawford. But the apex of the V was found to be strongly entrenched and admitted of no thoroughfare between it and the river, so that both forces were obliged to fall back.

Repulses from Ox Ford May 24. It was then about noon, and at this juncture the ford at Quarles Mill, 1½ miles above Ox Ford, was discovered. Thereupon Burnside sent one of his two divisions (Crittenden's) to cross by Quarles Mill and to join Crawford in a renewed attempt to push back the apex of the V. The other division (Wilcox's) of the IX Corps waited opposite the

Ox Ford for an opportunity to cross.[1] From Hancock's side Potter's division of the IX Corps and two brigades were to renew the attack on the apex from below.

But all Grant's efforts to establish communication between his two wings ended in failure. Crittenden was repulsed with heavy loss and Crawford fared the same. There were no guns with this force, and Crawford lost connexion with the rest of his corps. Both divisions fell back in some disorder. Potter's force also was repulsed but his losses were less severe.

In the afternoon Hancock was ordered to test the strength of Anderson's defence, and at 6 p.m. Gibbon's division with other troops in support attacked the Confederate right. But the position, consisting of heavy earthworks, faced with formidable abatis, was too strong to give any prospect of success, and the assault was discontinued.

Meanwhile the VI Corps had crossed at Jericho Mills in the morning and prolonged the right of the V Corps, but neither this corps nor the two right Divisions of the V Corps came into action this day. Detachments of the VI Corps, however, destroyed the railway on the 24th and 25th.

On the evening of the 24th one Federal division only remained north of the river opposite Ox Ford. The rest of the army was divided by Lee's works into two bodies; the one consisting of one corps and one division,

[1] Ferrero's coloured division was with the trains.

and the other of two corps and one division. They remained thus throughout the 25th and 26th, inviting destruction by a combination against one or other.

Grant's Artillery. When Grant withdrew from Spottsylvania on the 20th he sent back ninety-two guns to Washington, finding himself encumbered by artillery. When we read that Crittenden and Crawford on the 24th were unsupported by guns and that the assaults on Cold Harbour were largely repulsed by artillery fire, and note that Grant seems to have relied almost entirely on his infantry in the attack, it must be said that the Federal general was not an expert in the employment of artillery At North Anna the reduction of the Federal artillery nearly equalized the artillery for both sides. Lee had about 190 guns and Grant about 220.

Lee's Opportunity at North Anna. Had Lee then massed his whole artillery with Hill's corps and at the apex of the position, it should have rendered that side of the works secure from attack and might even have released a portion of the troops holding it. He would then have had two corps available with which to fall upon the II Corps with its supplementary division of the IX. Only the division of the IX Corps at Ox Ford was available for immediate reinforcement, for those on the Federal right would have had to march eight miles and cross the river twice. Hancock's only line of retrea twas by the Telegraph Road bridge, as the swamp barred movement to his left. It seems scarcely possible that he could have maintained himself against the combined assault of Ewell and Anderson. The destruction of Hancock's Corps would at least have deprived Grant for a time of the superiority in numbers necessary to continue operations against defensive positions, and might have resulted in the withdrawal of the army of the Potomac.

Why Lee did not avail himself of this magnificent opportunity is a problem that has been much debated.

There is, however, another problem which arises out of Lee's choice of his position. The works covered Ox Ford, but were drawn back from the bridge below it and from the fords above it. This, coupled with the fact that Hancock was allowed to cross without opposition suggests that Lee was inviting his enemy on to the south bank in order to entrap him. But his censure of Hill for allowing the V Corps to cross upsets this theory, as also does his failure to attack either of the Federal wings.

It then becomes a matter for wonder as to why he chose a position which did not defend the crossings and why he allowed the Virginia Central railway to be destroyed on his left. One solution which suggests itself to these two problems is that Lee hoped that his mere presence in this position would deter the Federal army from attempting to force a passage there, and that for some reason he did not intend to fight on the North Anna.

The explanation advanced by the Confederate writers is that Lee was in ill health, and on the 24th and 25th confined to his tent. As this was probably one of the first attacks of the heart affection from which he died five years later there is no doubt that he was temporarily incapacitated. But on the other hand he was well enough to ride on the 23rd, and his plans for attack, if he had any, would have been concieved on that day. But again it may have been that he had such plans and feared to risk a defeat so near the capital by entrusting so important a movement to his subordinates. Collapse which accompanies heart complaints would account for mental as well as physical incapacity.

However, Grant's interpretation of Lee's inaction, which he stated with the completest conviction, was based on what he reports to be the unanimous statements of prisoners. It was to the effect that the army of Virginia was morally beaten, and that the troops could not be induced to take the offensive outside their works. This, however, is not borne out by the subsequent actions of that army, though it is possible that the troops were wearied.

Withdrawal of Federal Army. On the 25th Grant began his preparation for withdrawing from his predicament, and succeeded in doing so unobserved. Wilson's cavalry division was sent to make a diversion on the Little River, which caused Lee to report that a movement seemed to be contemplated round his left flank. At the same time both the V and II Corps were ordered to menace the position. Provision was also made to alleviate the disadvantages of the situation by laying extra bridges and making roads on the north bank to facilitate communication between the two wings of the army.

During the night of the 25th the right division of the VI Corps was withdrawn across the river and posted in concealment, its position being occupied by a skeleton force. The trains also crossed that night.

Orders for the withdrawal were issued on the morning of the 26th, but the troops did not move till nightfall. The VI Corps moved first, and was followed by the V. The IX and II Corps followed last, leaving strong rear guards which were withdrawn at the last moment.

No attempt was made by the Confederates to interfere with the movement, which appears to have escaped detection.

The Federal losses from the 20th to the 26th were 1,143. Lee's casualties were probably slight.

TOTOPOTOMOY

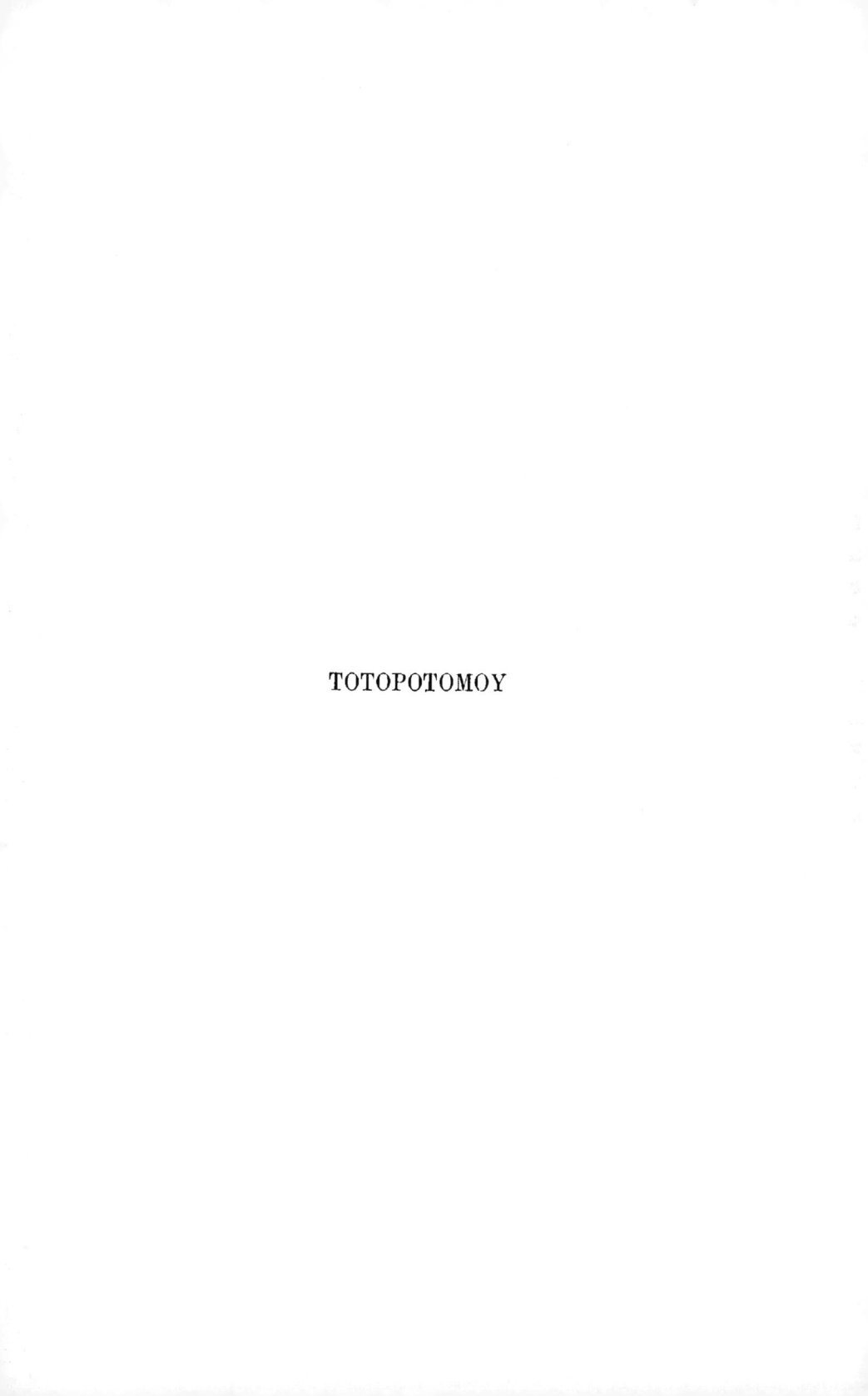

CHAPTER IX

TOTOPOTOMOY

GRANT'S withdrawal from the North Anna was in no way a retrograde movement. His despatches show that his intention was to move round the Confederates right at Hanover Junction, and that he would have done so but for the Sexton Marsh which barred his progress by that flank. He therefore had no choice but to recross the river and make the passage lower down. The next crossing indicated was obviously below the confluence of the North and South Annas, which combined seven miles below the Hanover Junction bridges to form the Pamunkey River. About four miles below the junction of the streams lies Hanover Court House on the south bank, with two fords leading to it three miles apart.

It appears that Lee thought at first that Hanover Court House was Grant's destination when he retired from Hanover Junction, for in his dispatch to Richmond reporting the withdrawal of the enemy he only mentions Ashland Station as the point to which he intended to transfer his own army. It soon became evident, however, that Hanover Town, twelve miles below the Court House, was the objective of the Federal army.

The routes from either point to Richmond were approximately equal, but the lower point was preferred as being nearer the new base at White House on the York River. On the advance from Spottsylvania the base was changed from Fredricksburg to Port Royal, and on the retirement from North Anna this was also abandoned and the train of 4,000 waggons was dispatched via Bowling Green to refill at White House.

Federal Movements, May 26. On the night of the 26th the Federal corps marched from their positions on the south bank of the North Anna and pushed on throughout that night and the next day towards Hanover Town.

The VI Corps, which was the first to be withdrawn, headed the march on the roads nearest the river

The V Corps marched abreast of it further north.

The II Corps followed the VI with the IX Corps on its left behind the V Corps.

On the night of the 27th Grant's headquarters halted at Maggahick Church, twenty-two miles from Jericho Ford, and the head of the VI Corps was within 3 miles of Hanover Ferry.

On the afternoon of the 26th Sheridan, with Gregg and Torbert's division, had moved down the river with the object of securing a crossing over the Pamunkey in advance of the army. Russell's division of the VI Corps, which withdrew from North Anna on the night of the 25th, followed them in support. An attempt was made to mislead the enemy into thinking that Hanover Court House was the threatened point by menacing the fords opposite it. Gregg attacked at Little Page Ford and Torbert at Taylor's Ford during the 26th evening, and left some of their force there during the night to continue the demonstrations, but at nightfall the main bodies pushed on to Hanover Town to seize the passage there.

On the morning of the 27th Torbert's division crossed and encountered some resistance from Gordon's brigade of cavalry. After a sharp skirmish, in which Russell's infantry participated, the Confederates were driven out of the town with a loss of thirty or forty prisoners, and were followed up to Crump's Creek by the cavalry. The infantry halted near the crossing.

Lee's Movements, May 27. Meanwhile Lee had not been slow in conforming to the new move. At 6.45 a.m. on the 27th he was informed by wire of the passage of Sheridan's force at Hanover Town, which revealed Grant's intention of using that crossing.

Ewell's corps, commanded by Early (Ewell being ill), started almost as soon as the II Corps was off the ground and crossed the South Anna by the Virginia Central Railway bridge. Passing through Altees Station about noon the 28th, he took up a position that afternoon with his left on the Totopotomoy Creek about Pole Green

Church and his right near Bever Dam Creek on the Old Church road about a mile from Bethesda Church

Totopotomoy Position. Anderson's Corps followed close behind, and crossing the South Anna by the Fredricksburg railway bridge, was posted behind Early with two divisions, (Field and Kershaw,) on the Shady Grove Church road [1] and the third (Pickett) near the old Church road. Between Early's left and Breckenridge's division, which came next in line, there existed a gap of about a mile.

Kershaw's and Field's division were in rear of this gap, and both Kershaw and Breckenridge were in some anxiety on account of it. Lee, however, evidently anticipating the possibility of further manœuvring on the part of the enemy, was anxious to keep a force intact for use on his right if necessary, and relied on the fact that the country where the gap occurred and also that portion of the Totopotomoy Creek opposite to it presented natural obstacles. At the Cold Harbour position five weeks later he again left gaps in his line to be defended by physical obstructions, and his skill in thus availing him-

---

[1] Humphreys places Anderson on Early's right; Badeau puts him on the left of the whole line; the above is taken from Official Records, Series I, vol. xxxv., part iii., pp. 844 *et seq.*, in which Kershaw's despatch to headquarters, drawing attention to the gap between Early and Breckenridge, gives a sketch map showing the position of his own and Field's division on the Shady Grove Church Road. Pickett's division is not located, and probably was behind Early's right. Messages from headquarters to Breckenridge state that Anderson was "well closed up" in rear of Early, with orders to be ready to support him on either side.

self of every advantage of the ground contributed largely towards enabling him to hold his attenuated line.

Hill's corps was on Breckenridge's left and extended along the creek to the Virginia Central Railway, where his line was about a mile in advance of Altees Station.

The whole army was in position on the night of the 28th.

The country between the Pamunkey River and Richmond is low lying and there are few eminences. The streams run between marshy banks and swamps occur frequently. The region is covered with patches of dwarf jungle and stunted woods. From Hanover Town a main road runs south-west through Hawes Shop to Meadow Bridge over the Chikahominy River at the eleventh mile. From Hawes Shop a road lies south-east to Old Church and thence eastwards to White House. From this road, at a point two and a half miles from Hawes Shop, the Mechanicsville Road runs generally WSW. through Bethseda Church to Mechanicsville Bridge. The northern defences of Richmond covered these two bridges. From Hanover Town a third road passed through Old Church to Cold Harbour generally southwards, and then south-west through Gaines Mill to New Bridge, three and a half miles distant from the Richmond defences. The next bridge, Bottom's Bridge, over the Chikahominy is nine miles lower down the stream and twelve miles east of Richmond. Owing to the swampy nature of its banks the stream was a formidable obstacle and not to be crossed save by bridging. Lee, therefore, was now finally interposed before Richmond, and Grant likewise had reached the point whence manœuvres would bring him no nearer his goal. He now had to break through the Army of Virginia or else recede down the Chikahominy to make a fresh attempt from the east or south.

On the forenoon of the 28th, while the Confederate corps were moving into position, the Federal army crossed the Pamunkey. The VI and II Corps crossed four miles above Hanover Town and the V at Hanover Ferry. A line was formed about one and a half miles from the river, the II Corps being in the centre. The IX Corps remained on the north bank, while the cavalry were in advance on the Meadow Bank Road.

The position of the Confederate army was unknown, and Grant was in doubt as to whether or not Lee would be met north of the Chikahaminy. Sheridan was consequently sent out on the Meadow Bridge Road to elucidate the situation. He was not, however, able to proceed far, for the Southern cavalry, supported by infantry, were found holding Hawes Shop and until evening defied all attempts to dislodge them. A sharp fight ensued, without advantage to either side until Custer's brigade joined in the attack. The Federal troopers then charged, dismounted and carried the defences. But the reconnaissance was abandoned and Sheridan fell back behind the

Sheridan's Reconnaissance. Hawes Shop.

infantry, who were close in rear. He had lost 350 men. Wilson's cavalry had remained on the north bank to protect the trains, for whose safety there was always considerable apprehension. He did not cross till the morning of the 30th.

During the 28th Lee's headquarters were at Altees Station. This circumstance combined with his subsequent attacks on the Federal right seem to indicate that he at one time expected the issue to take place in that part of the field.

Federal Reconnaissance in Force, May 29. On the 29th the position of the enemy being still unknown Grant ordered a reconnaissance in force. The VI Corps moved up the river as far as Hanover Court House but found no enemy. This shows how effectually the Confederate cavalry had screened the main position. The II and V Corps moved against the Totopotomoy Creek and the IX Corps crossed the Pamunkey River and was placed between them in reserve at Hawes Shop.

The II Corps advancing along the Meadow Bridge Road came upon Hill and Breckenridge strongly posted behind the upper waters of the creek. Griffin's division of the V Corps crossed the stream about opposite Hawes Shop and began to move down the Shady Grove Church road. The enemy being found in force on this flank, Cutler's division also crossed to support Griffin.

It now became evident that Lee's army was in position

L

behind the Totopotomoy, and as the VI Corps was absent no further advance was made. There was energetic skirmishing but no serious fighting that day. The strength displayed on the Confederate right caused Grant to fear a possible offensive movement from that side, and Sheridan with two divisions of cavalry was sent to watch that flank.

Indeed the position of the V Corps across the creek was a dangerous one, as it was within easy reach of both Early and Anderson, and presented just such an opportunity as Jackson used repeatedly to turn to account. Had the V Corps been severely handled and driven back across the creek it would have become more difficult for Grant to establish connection with White House, and his reinforcements from that place would have been obliged to make a long detour via Hanover Town instead of approaching via Old Church as they did. It was by such counter-strokes as these that the weak Virginian Army had sustained the war for so long. But Stonewall Jackson, the initiator and exponent of these tactics, was dead, and now it seemed that the spirit he had brought to the army on his first field at Bull Run was also passing. Lee himself must have been influenced by the failure of any of his lieutenants to emulate Jackson's achievements, and there is no doubt that the almost simultaneous loss of Longstreet and Stuart seriously affected him, as it did the rest of the army. In defence the Confederate soldiers were as steadfast as ever, as is evinced by the combat in the Wilderness and the recapture of the angle at Spottsylvania, but it seemed now to have been, as Grant opined, that Lee fought only to prolong the struggle and without hope of winning the war in the field.

Action of Totopotomoy, May 30.
On the 30th the Federals resumed their advance. The VI Corps was recalled from Hanover Court House to the right of the II Corps, and was to outflank the enemy's left, forming across it if possible. But in returning across the marshes and swamps about Crump's Creek, it was greatly delayed and only arrived on the field at nightfall, too late to participate in the operations of that day. The II Corps crossed the Totopotomoy and had some fighting with the outposts of Breckenridge and Hill, but did not seriously attempt to assault the main works, which were exceedingly strong. The IX Corps crossed the creek on the right of the V Corps about Witlock House and extended towards the Shady Grove Church road facing Early's left and centre. There was brisk skirmishing, but no headway was made owing to the strength of the resistance encountered. The V Corps advanced up the Shady Grove Church road until it came upon Early's right, which was drawn across the road and posted behind a difficult ravine. Griffin's division was leading, followed by Cutler and Crawford. On observing Warren's approach, which threatened to overlap his right, Early transferred Rodes' division from his left and sent it

round by Bethesda Church to fall on the left on the V Corps. Rodes' place was taken by Field's division of Anderson's corps. Throughout the day the Federal skirmishers on the south of the Shady Grove Church road had been engaged with parties of Lee's cavalry, so that Rodes' advance was screened and he fell upon the divisions of Cutler and Crawford unawares and drove them back some distance. But the Federal troops were soon rallied and beat off a very resolute assault, after which Rodes having lost severely was obliged to withdraw. Fearing that Lee might follow up this advantage, Grant ordered an assault by the II Corps to create a diversion. Hancock attacked with vigour and captured the first lines of rifle pits in front of Breckenridge. He was unable to make further progress, but succeeded in holding the ground he had gained in spite of several attempts to dislodge him. Meanwhile Warren had brought more of his troops into line and advanced against Rodes, driving him back about a mile and a half and occupying Bethesda Church.

The measure of the resistance encountered on the 30th led Grant to anticipate a repetition of his experiences at Spottsylvania Court House, for the next day he wrote to Washington asking that all available bridging material and transportation should be sent to the James river in view of the advisability of transferring the Potomac army to the south of that river. Thus we see that while the Southerners had ceased to bid for victory yet their aspect was still so formidable that Grant, notwithstanding his numbers and the admirable behaviour of his troops, was beginning to despair of defeating the army of Virginia in the field, and was already contemplating siege operations against the southern defences of the capital.

On hearing of Butler's reverse on the 15th and his subsequent incarceration in Bermudah Hundred, Grant had written to Washington stating that Butler was not detaining 10,000 men in Richmond, and asking that all his troops which were not required to hold his lines should be sent at once to White House. Butler declared that he was detaining a force more than equal to his own, in which of course he was utterly mistaken. He, however, on receipt of the orders, promptly dispatched half his army consisting of 15,000 men under Smith, although he was at that moment starting to make an attempt on Petersburg from City Point, which, considering how weakly the place was then held, ought to have had a good chance of success. It may here be observed that Butler was first set the impossible task of blockading Richmond on the south bank of the James, and then "hustled" because he did not immediately retrieve an error not entirely his own. The same treatment was meted out later on to Thomas, because he insisted on taking his own time in dealing with Hood's army at Nashville, and, on the very day that he fell upon

Arrival of XVIII Corps at White House.

that army and annihilated it, the officer detailed to supersede him arrived in the town.

Grant, on being informed of Smith's arrival at White House on May 30, ordered him to march without delay to Old Church. Smith, though his ships only arrived at 11 a.m., disembarked and started the same evening without waiting for baggage, rations, or even reserve ammunition, and reached Old Church on the night of the 31st. He left a division at White House to guard the base, and had some 13,000 men with him. His force became known as the XVIII Corps.

Smith was also informed that he was in considerable danger, as the enemy might make an attempt to cut him off by moving towards Old Church. Grant, however, stated that Smith should not avoid an encounter, as nothing could suit him better than such a movement of the enemy, for he intended in that event to advance his right and endeavour to interpose between him and Richmond.

Dispositions on May 30. On the night of the 30th the V Corps lay between the Shady Grove and Mechanicsville roads, three miles south of the Totopotomoy (its left about Bethesda Church). The IX Corps continued the line rather north of westwards, with the II Corps on its right along the south bank of the Totopotomoy Creek.

The VI Corps, after emerging from the bogs of Crump's Creek, had reached the Meadow Bridge road about a mile north of the Totopotomoy.

Lee's lines reached from Altees Station to the Mechanicsville road where Pickett had come up on Early's right. During the day Hoke's Division had arrived from Richmond and was posted behind the right, where Kershaw's Division also stood in reserve.

On the 30th Sheridan, with the divisions of Gregg and Torbert, was north of the Matadequin Creek, guarding the approach from White House. At about 1 p.m., observing a Confederate cavalry force (FitzHugh Lee) on the south bank he moved out and attacked it, driving it back to Cold Harbour.

Grant had evidently intended to fight in the position he held on the 30th, for up to the 31st he issued no orders for a move elsewhere. But late on that day an advantage gained by Sheridan determined him to make a strenuous effort against the enemy's extreme right and to force his way through it to the Chikahominy.

COLD HARBOUR

CHAPTER X

Cold Harbour

ON the morning of the 31st May, Sheridan advanced from behind Matadequin Creek, in the direction of Cold Harbour, in order to find Lee's right. These villages were found to be held by FitzHugh Lee's cavalry with detachments of Anderson's infantry in support behind log breastworks. As the enemy did not appear to be in superior force the Federals attacked vigorously, and after some severe fighting gained possession of the works late in the afternoon. As this movement threatened to turn the right flank of the Confederates, Anderson at once sent Kershaw's Division to retake the place, and on seeing a strong force of infantry approaching, Sheridan commenced to withdraw. His troops had actually evacuated the works when a message arrived from Grant ordering that Cold Harbour should be held at all costs. The breastworks were again manned and preparations made to defend them to the last.

Sheridan seizes Cold Harbour.

During the night of the 31st the assaulting columns moved into position to attack the place at dawn.

Movements towards Cold Harbour. As soon as he heard of Sheridan's success Grant ordered the VI Corps (then on the extreme right) to march with all speed to Cold Harbour. The distance was nine miles and difficulties of a night march delayed them en route, so that Wright did not arrive till 9 a.m. on June 1. At the same time as Grant determined to make good Sheridan's advantage, Lee resolved to re-establish his right at Cold Harbour, and Anderson's corps was ordered to move to the right to occupy the villages.

At dawn on June 1 while the two corps were marching, Kershaw's division assaulted Sheridan's works, but were repulsed with severe loss. They renewed the attack soon after, but with the same result, the fire of the cavalry, supported by their horse artillery, being too strong for the assailants.

At 9 a.m. the VI Corps began to arrive and Anderson abandoned the attempt to retake the villages, falling back to a strong position opposite them.

Warren's left overlapped Early's right, so that at daybreak on June 1 Anderson's columns were observed passing before the left of the V Corps. Grant immediately ordered Warren to attack them in flank, while Wright was directed to advance from Cold Harbour and assail the head of the columns. Both failed, however, to carry out the scheme. Warren opened with artillery, and at 3 p.m. reported that the breastworks were very strong, and his own line so attenuated that he could not muster an assaulting column. Wright sent out skirmishing lines and delayed till 2 p.m., so that by the time the Federal infantry moved forward Anderson's whole Corps was strongly entrenched in front of Warren and Wright.

Failure to turn Lee's Right.

At the same time as the VI Corps was despatched from the right, Smith, who was at Old Church on the night of June 31, was also ordered to march on Cold Harbour and co-operate with the V and VI Corps. Through a clerical error the name, Newcastle, was substituted for Cold Harbour, and thinking a battle was imminent, Smith hurried his troops thither without waiting for breakfast, only to find that his orders were obviously mistaken. At Newcastle corrected orders reached him and he hastened southwards. The weather was intensely hot and the dust heavy, so that the troops who were unaccustomed to marching, fell out in large numbers Smith did not reach his position between the V and VI Corps till 3 p.m. and then with only 10,000 men out of 13,000

Grant was greatly disappointed by this failure, as he had conceived great hopes that the whole of the Confederate right would have been broken up while on the move by a vigorous offensive on the part of the V, VI, and XVIII Corps.

Cold Harbour Position. The position to which the Confederate right had fallen back after their unsuccessful effort to regain Cold Harbour was one of the strongest they had ever occupied. From about one and a half miles west of Cold Harbour a ridge runs nearly south to the Chikahominy, where it terminates in an impassable morass on the river bank. The slopes at the north end of the ridge were intersected by ravines, but those towards Cold Harbour were long and gradual. The parapets occupied the crest of the rise, and some distance in front a sunken road furnished an advanced line of defence. The ridge was crowned with pine woods, but in front of it lay a strip of clearing 300 to 12,000 yards broad.

First Attack on Cold Harbour, June 1. To meet the menace to his right Lee had transferred Hoke's division to the ridge and placed it on Anderson's right. Against this position Wright and Smith advanced at 5 p.m. on June 1, and delivered a well-ordered and powerful attack. The clearings were crossed in spite of heavy loss and the position gained. Rickett's division of the VI Corps penetrated between Hoke and Kershaw, who was on Anderson's right, and captured 500 prisoners. Wright reported that he hoped to seize the works up to the Chikahominy, but he was over-sanguine, and it was found impossible to make any impression on the second line of breastworks which had been thrown up to bar his progress. However, he retained the position he had won, in spite of a determined effort to evict him.

Smith's corps carried the advanced lines of Anderson's centre, which lay in a strip of fir woods, but on attempting to reach the main position across a second clearing he was repulsed with heavy loss. His right did not connect with the V Corps, and it came under a heavy enfilade fire of guns from eminences on the north end of the ridge. He, however, had taken 250 prisoners and was able to retain the ground he had gained. The losses of the VI and XVIII Corps in these assaults were 2,200.

Diversions against Federal Right. Meanwhile, in order to prevent Grant from exerting more force at Cold Harbour, Lee attacked all along the rest of the line. Early went out against Warren three times, but was each time repulsed with heavy loss. Hill and Breckenridge attacked the II and IX Corps, but with no better fortune.

During the night of the 1st Hoke and Anderson also made several attempts to regain the lost ground, but without effect.

The success gained on his left determined Grant to press his advantage there. Soon after dark on the night of the 1st the II Corps was withdrawn from the right and sent to prolong the left of the VI Corps up to the Chikahominy. The night was dark and the roads unknown, and Hancock's troops lost their way and fell into confusion. They were reunited, however, and reached their station, twelve miles distant, at 6.30 a.m. A general attack had been ordered for daybreak, June 2, but as the II Corps had been moving all night and the men were exhausted by heat and want of food, the attack was postponed till 5 p.m. Further developments caused it to be postponed till next morning.

Confederate Dispositions, June 2. As soon as Lee became aware that the II Corps had moved from the front, he appreciated Grant's intention and transferred two divisions (Mahone and Wilcox) of Hill's Corps and Breckenridge's division to Hoke's right to extend the line to the Chikahominy. Heth's division of Hill's corps remained on the left of Early. Pickett's division was on Anderson's left, Field's in his centre and Kershaw's on his right. But three brigades from Field's division were placed behind Kershaw's right, as the front which they had occupied was covered by an impassable swamp. Lee's troops were then in the following order from the left: Heth's division and Early's corps forming the left wing; the divisions of Pickett, Kershaw and Field in the centre, and the divisions of Hoke, Mahone, Wilcox, and Breckenridge on the right.

Early's Attack on Federal Right, June 2 During the morning of the 2nd Warren was ordered to extend his left to connect with the XVIII Corps and to contract his front so that it could be held by half the corps, with the rest in reserve. The IX Corps was

COLD HARBOUR

withdrawn and ordered to form in mass behind the right of the V Corps to resist an attempt to outflank the right of the line and to support the V Corps if necessary. The support was needed, for as soon as Burnside moved Early and Heth sallied out and attacked him and the right of the V Corps.

Lee seems to have concluded that Burnside was moving to the Federal left, for he directed Early to form across the flank of the V Corps and sweep down the line. Early attempted to do so, and succeeded in outflanking the V Corps and taking several hundred prisoners, but was checked by their reserves and by the IX Corps. Severe fighting continued till nightfall, but without advantage to either side, except that Lee's left had now swung forward and rested on the Totopotomoy and Grant's right was withdrawn to Bethesda Church. Both armies extended to the Chikahominy.

Grant was extremely annoyed that Burnside and Warren had not made a counter-attack on Early when he emerged from the works, for the one consummation he desired was the opportunity of meeting the Confederate troops in the open. He did not hear what had happened until it was over, but he thereupon issued a special order that commanders were to attack the enemy whenever he left cover. The fault of his generals was undoubtedly a lack of initiative and a too great dependence on orders. The actions of all of them except Hancock gave evidence of this.

In consequence of these attacks on the Federal right the assault on Lee's right ordered for the afternoon of the 2nd was postponed till the following morning

Cavalry Movements, June 2, 3. On June 2 Wilson's cavalry division returned from its mission of destroying the railways between the North Anna and Richmond and took post on the Federal right. Sheridan had been ordered to co-operate in the assault on Anderson and Hoke by attacking their flank and rear, but his orders failed to reach him in time, and on the 3rd he crossed to the south of the river to reconnoitre the roads southwards. The Confederate cavalry on the 2nd had also passed to the south side of the Chikahominy and were watching the roads to the James for any movement in that direction.

Final Assaults at Cold Harbour. Before ordering his frontal attack on Cold Harbour, Grant was much exercised in mind as to whether it would be justified after the experience of the Wilderness and Spottsylvania, for the strength of the Confederate positions promised very heavy losses. The impatience of the Government and populace at the duration of the struggle, the cost of the war, which amounted to 4,000,000 [1] dollars a day, added to his own reluctance and that of the army to abandon without a final effort the task on which they had expended so much blood and labour—all these considerations combined

[1] Porter.

to persuade him against his instinctive judgment. Grant was not alone in his anticipations of slaughter, for many of the soldiers of the assaulting column before going into action pinned their names and home addresses on to the back of their coats. Grant stated that this was the only action he ever regretted having fought.

At 4.30 a.m. on June 3 the II and VI and XVIII Corps assaulted Lee's line in front of Cold Harbour. The commanders of the V and IX Corps were ordered to co-operate against the works in front of them " in such a manner and with such combinations as their judgment dictated, taking advantage of any weakness which might appear."

Assault by II Corps. The II Corps advanced with the divisions of Barlow and Gibbon in the front line. Forcing their way through swamps and tangled brushwood in the face of a heavy fire, Barlow's division reached the sunken road which formed the first line of Breckenridge's position, and drove out the defenders in confusion, taking several hundred prisoners and three guns, which were turned on the enemy. The second line, however, failed to arrive in time to support Barlow, and a counter-attack from the main position, aided by an enfilade fire of guns, forced him back out of the captured trench with heavy losses. His troops, however, behaved in the most determined manner, and taking advantage of a slight rise fifty yards distant from the sunken road, they entrenched themselves there under a heavy fire. On Barlow's right the ranks of Gibbon's division were broken up by ravines and an impassable morass divided his command. But the regiments struggled forward with the greatest heroism, and in some places detachments even gained parapets. But nowhere were they able to remain. Gibbon several times renewed the assault, but was totally unable to make headway against the terrific fire of musketry and artillery which met all his efforts to advance.

The Confederate position had two slight salients which were used as bastions and heavily gunned One projecting behind the II and VI Corps brought an enfilade fire on Hancock's right, and on the left of the line formed by Wright and Smith. The other salient was on Smith's right and enfiladed his line and Wright's from that side, so that a cross-fire was brought on to those two corps.

Assaults by VI and XVIII Corps. The VI Corps advanced at the same time as Hancock and succeeded in gaining a line of rifle pits, but although gallant attempts were made to reach the main works they were all repulsed with great slaughter.

The XVIII Corps had been subjected to so severe an artillery fire from its right that Smith decided to make his advance up a ravine which led up to the centre of the portion of the position allotted to him. This enabled him to reach and take the Confederate rifle pits, but on emerging from this cover to reform his line the severity of the cross-fire made it impossible to advance until the VI Corps could divert some of it from him. His divisions were ordered to wait until the VI Corps had made more progress, but the centre division, Martindale's, mistaking the firing of the VI Corps for the advance of the left division of its own corps, rushed forward with the greatest courage, and made three assaults, all of which were repulsed with the heaviest loss.

Smith thereupon reported that he was unable to advance without Wright's support to divert the fire from his left. Wright had just reported that he was waiting for Smith, so both were ordered to repeat their assaults. Smith's troops had been terribly cut up, but he formed a new column of his last four regiments and waited for an opportunity to attack. Before that came, however, Grant had ordered the cessation of the assault.

In the Federal centre the V Corps being still greatly extended was not able to effect much, but an advance was made and several rifle pits captured. The IX Corps fared rather better, and moving on to the right of the V drove back Early's left from some of the positions they had captured the day before, but they, too, were checked by artillery fire. Wilson's cavalry, who were beyond Early's left, tried to connect with Burnside, but were intercepted and forced back to Hawes Shop.

Assaults by V and IX Corps.

The first onslaught on Lee's right lasted less than an hour and the main attack here

Assaults Abandoned.

had virtually come to an end at 7 a.m., although spasmodic efforts were made to renew it for several hours later. At 11 a.m. Grant rode down the line to consult with the corps commanders as to the advisability of continuing the assault. Hancock and Warren were of opinion that the position could not be taken, and Smith was very doubtful of success. Wright thought that he might get in if supported on both flanks. Burnside only was sanguine. Consequently at 1.30 p.m. the order was issued to desist from attack and to strengthen the positions which had been won.

It is often stated that the Federal troops refused to obey the orders to continue the assaults after the first repulse, but even Lee in his report speaks of " repeated assaults." The despatches and orders do not show that any peremptory order was given, and Grant's order at 7 a.m. was to the effect that the attack should be suspended the moment it became certain that it could not succeed. The statement seems founded on Smith's reply to his orders in which he stated that he could not advance without support. Hancock made a distinct second assault about noon on his own initiative.

It is also notable that Grant does not seem to have made any special disposition of artillery to support the attack, and certainly no artillery preparation. Smith, when he found himself checked mostly by shell fire, had to send for guns with which to reply, and Burnside on the right made the same demand when repulsed by Early. Both cases indicate that no artillery support was prearranged.

Although the Federals in this battle were repulsed with great slaughter in a very short space of time they were very near achieving a great success. Lee said to a member of Davis' cabinet on the field that he had not a single regiment in reserve, and added that if he shortened his line to make one he would be outflanked, while if he weakened it the enemy would break through. This disposes of certain criticisms made to the effect that Lee should have counter attacked upon Grant's defeated troops.

There is little doubt that in this battle Lee owed much to his skilful disposition and employment of his guns, and that Grant failed to avail himself to the full of the assistance of that arm.

The Federal losses for May 28-31, were about 3,000 in killed, wounded and missing On June 1, they lost about 3,500, and on June 3 about 7,000. Lee's casualties are unknown, but were far less severe, probably about 4,000 or 5,000 for the period May 27 to June 12.

Grant's losses from May 4 to June 12 were estimated by him at 54,926. Those of Lee have never been accurately compiled, but are generally given at about 30,000.

From June 3 till June 12 the armies confronted each other in their positions on places only 40 yards apart. Porter gives a lucid description of the situation. " Every attempt to make a change in the picket line brought on heavy firing, as both sides had become nervous from long watchfulness, and the slightest movement on either front led to the belief that it was the beginning of an assault. In the night there was often heavy artillery firing accompanied by musketry, with a view to deterring the other side from attacking, or occasioned by false rumours of an attempt to assault. The men on the advanced lines had to lie close to the ground in narrow trenches, with little water except from surface drainage In places a distance of 30 or 40 yards was completely covered by the dead . . . the stench became sickening."

Grant maintained this proximity in order to deter Lee from detaching a force against Hunter, who was advancing down the valley, and his menacing attitude answered the purpose of more offensive measures. But, unfortunately for Hunter, Grant's impatience to proceed with his own operations led him to move on just at the critical moment when Hunter was leaving Staunton for Lynchburg, with the result that Hunter fell a victim to the force liberated by Grant's withdrawal on the 12th.

On June 6 Early made a second attempt against Grant's right from North of Matadequin Creek. It failed on account of his troops becoming involved in the swamps about the Creek. He repeated the attempt next day from the South of the Creek, but with the same result.

On June 7 Sheridan started to co-operate with Hunter towards Charlotteville, but finding he had taken another route and being assailed by the Confederate cavalry at Trevylian Station he fell back with a loss of 1,500 men and returned to headquarters.

On June 9 works were erected on the right rear and along the bank of the Chikahominy to prevent interference with the withdrawal of the army, and on June 12 Grant commenced to transfer the army of the Potomac to the south of the James to try " the back door of Petersburg."

PETERSBURG

CHAPTER XI

PETERSBURG

GRANT'S design in transferring his army from Lee's front was to do so in such a manner as to bring an overwhelming force against Petersburg before Lee could anticipate him there. The greatest secrecy was observed as to the nature of the movement, and the destination was only known to a few of the highest officers.

Petersburg was a place of primary importance, being the convergence of three railways which connect Richmond with the south. The loss of it would have rendered Richmond untenable.

Move to the James, June 13. On the night of June 12 Smith's corps marched to White House to embark there, and rejoin Butler's command at Bermudah Hundred.

At the same time a brigade of Wilson's cavalry division proceeded to the Long Bridge over the Chikahominy, fifteen miles down stream from Cold Harbour, to prepare a crossing there. All the bridges had been destroyed, and the south bank was held only by weak cavalry pickets, nearly the whole of FitzHugh Lee's and Hampton's divisions having followed Sheridian towards Charlottesville.

Wilson had no difficulty in forcing a passage, and laying a pontoon, over which the V Corps, followed by the II, crossed on the morning of the 13th.

The IX Corps, followed by the VI, crossed soon after at Jones Bridge, five miles lower down and the trains crossed lower still.

The V Corps moved at once to hold the bridges over the White Oak swamp and was instructed to demonstrate as if to turn the Confederate right.

The II Corps pushed on by a forced march, and reached Wilcox Landing on the James on the afternoon of the 13th. The VI and IX Corps arrived there next day.

Lee's Movements, June 13-17. Lee did not discover the withdrawal of the army from his front until the morning of the 13th, when he immediately sent out skirmishers, and came upon the V Corps advancing from White Oak Swamp. He at once assumed a renewal of Grant's movements round his right, and moved the corps of Anderson and Hill to cover Washington from White Oak to Malvern Hill.

On the same day he resolved to detach Early's corps to defeat the movement against Lynchburg. He evidently considered that the terrible punishment inflicted on the enemy at Cold Harbour would deter him, for a time at any rate, from risking its repetition by making any serious effort against the stronger lines of Richmond. His instructions to Early were to recover the valley, and he gave him permission to make a raid against Washington at his discretion. By thus detaching this corps for an indefinite period, Lee clearly shows that he had decided to adopt a purely defensive attitude behind the Richmond defences. The fact that a military genius such as Lee should have resigned himself to the attitude which can never achieve victory, indicates that he had abandoned hope of winning the cause of the South in the field. The contemplated raid against Washington is further evidence of the policy which, while striving to avoid defeat, played to gain a specious success which might be used to induce the foreign intervention wherein the Government of the Confederacy already saw their only hope.

On the night of the 13th the V Corps retired on Wilcox Landing, reaching it on the afternoon of the 14th. Some skirmishing with its rear guard occurred on that day, but from then till the 17th Lee lost all trace of the army of the Potomac.

This is evidenced by his messages on June 17. At 12 noon he wired from Drewry Bluff, "Until I can get more definite information of Grant's movements I do not think it prudent to draw more troops to this side of the river." At 1.45 p.m. he wired, "Warren's troops crossed the Chikahominy at Long Bridge on the 13th.

... Some prisoners were taken from it (V Corps) on the 14th; have not heard of it since." At 4.30 he wired, "Have no information of Grant's crossing the James."

Passage of the II Corps. At Wilcox Landing the bridging material ordered by Grant on May 30 had arrived, and the bridge was commenced at 4 p.m. on the 14th and completed in seven hours. It was 700 yards long, and had 101 pontoons anchored to ships.

On the afternoon of the 14th the II Corps began to cross the river by ferry steamers to Windmill Point, the opposite point to Wilcox Landing on the south bank about fifteen miles from Petersburg. By daybreak, the 15th, the whole corps was across with four batteries. Butler had been ordered to send rations to meet the II Corps, and their non-arrival delayed Hancock till 10.30 a.m., when he started without them.

Smith's Attack on Petersburg, June 15. Meanwhile Smith's corps from White House had disembarked at Bermudah Hundred on the night of the 14th and, receiving 6,000 reinforcements from Butler's command, started on the morning of the 15th against the Petersburg defences via the south bank of the Appomatox, crossing at City Point.[1] His force was now about 14,000 infantry. Kautz' division of cavalry went with him.

The advance was impeded by dense thickets, and the Confederate pickets made a determined resistance. However, by 1 30 the outposts were driven in, and the main position revealed. Smith, hesitating to make a direct attack on unknown works, spent the afternoon in making a reconnaissance in force, which succeeded in exposing the weakness of the garrison by gaining the parapets at several points on the centre and left. At 7.30 p.m. the main attack was delivered, and was entirely successful. The defenders were driven back from a mile and a half of works (composed of seven redans with infantry parapets between them), with a loss of 4 guns and 316 prisoners. At 6.30 p.m Hancock's leading divisions were within a mile of Smith's rear, and at the end of the battle were well up and ready to pursue the advantage with a night advance. But Smith advised waiting for daylight, and the troops bivouacked in the captured lines.

It has been remarked by nearly all authorities that for some time after the battle of Cold Harbour there was a marked falling off in the vigour of the Federal attacks, when compared with their quality at the beginning of the campaign. The loss of so many veterans and officers and the addition of recruits of an inferior type made this inevitable, even without the deterrent influences of the constant and bloody repulses they had suffered.

The hesitancy of Smith therefore is comprehensible if not justifiable and it also does not appear that Hancock had any direct orders to assault without delay and at all hazards. Only such orders would have really justified a night attack into a series of permanent works.

Reinforcement of Petersburg. It was, of course, unknown to Smith that the garrison of Petersburg on that day was only 2,400 regular infantry and 2,000 cavalry, in addition to the local militia, composed of old men and boys.

On the night of the 15th Hoke's division reached Petersburg, and Beauregard who commanded the Richmond garrison withdrew B. R. Johnson's division from the lines across the neck of Bermudah Hundred, leaving only one brigade (Gracie's) to do its best to retain the other division of Butler. Before morning Gracie also was withdrawn, and his outposts alone remained. The night was employed by the Confederates in erecting a new line behind that captured by Smith's corps.

Passage of the James. By the morning of the 16th the remainder of the army of the Potomac was across the James. The IX Corps had crossed on the evening of the 15th, and by the morning of the 16th had come upon the left of the II Corps, which had taken post on the left of the XVIII Corps. The V Corps crossed on the morning of the 16th, and did not arrive before Petersburg till next day. The VI Corps remained by the bridge.

By morning of the 16th Beauregard had 14,000 men in Petersburg. These just sufficed to hold the lines facing east from the Appomotax to the Jerusalem Plank Road, but reinforcements were now rapidly being thrown in from the Army of Virginia.

PETERSBURG

Although Lee wired on the 17th that he had no information of Grant's movements, Beauregard was better informed, and on his demand he despatched Anderson's corps on the 16th. This dearth of information was due to the absence of almost the whole of the Southern cavalry, who were opposing Sheridian's movements against the Virginia Central railway at Trevylian Station.

Fighting at Bermudah Hundred. At daybreak on the 16th the retirement of the Confederates from before the lines at Bermudah Hundred was discovered, and a division of Butler's command under Terry advanced as far as the railway, and attempted to destroy it. But strong Confederate columns were now arriving on the railway, and Terry was obliged to fall back to the lines he had captured As soon as Grant heard of this he ordered two divisions of the VI Corps from the bridge [1] to reinforce Bermudah Hundred, and for a time anticipated that Lee might fall upon Butler with overwhelming forces. This apprehension, added to the fact that the IX Corps **Second Attack on Petersburg, June 16.** required rest after its night march, induced him to defer his attack on Petersburg till the afternoon of the 16th. On that morning accidents had delayed the movement of the divisions of the II Corps, so that nothing was done till 6 a.m., when Hancock moved forward two divisions which found the works in their front strongly

[1] These divisions arrived about noon on the 17th.

held. Grant arrived on the ground from City Point about that time, and ordered the postponement of the assault till 6 p.m.

At that hour Hancock attacked, supported on his right by two brigades of Smith, and on his left by two brigades of the IX Corps. The breach which Smith had made the day before was widened by the capture of one redan on the right and two on the left, but no very definite advantages seems to have been gained. Smith on the right had reported against the feasibility of an assault and was ordered to demonstrate only. During the night of the 16th the Confederates made attempts to recapture the lost works, but without success, and fell back to fresh lines thrown up behind them.

Third Attack on Petersburg, June 17. Before morning on the 17th the V Corps had arrived on the left of the IX, and at daybreak the attack was resumed. But instead of being a general assault, it appears that the only serious efforts were made by the IX Corps.

At dawn a rush by Potter's division captured a redoubt, 4 guns and 600 prisoners, taking a mile of works on Shand House Ridge, but found themselves faced by another line. At 3 p.m. Wilcox's division gained a position in advance of Potter, and at 8 p.m. Ledlies' division carried a portion of the main defences, but was immediately driven out. The V Corps does not seem to have participated, except to send supports to assist in holding the captured works. Birney had assumed command of the II Corps, replacing Hancock, who was incapacitated by an old wound, and he seems to have lacked his chief's vigour. Nothing much was done by either the II or XVIII Corps, except that they established themselves somewhat nearer the enemies' works.

Bermudah Hundred, June 17.
On the 17th, Pickett's division which had arrived that morning at Drewry Bluff, attacked and retook from Butler the Confederate works across the neck of Bermudah Hundred. Field's division followed Pickett's, and proceeded to Petersburg. Pickett remained before Bermudah Hundred, but on that day Kershaw's division and the whole of Hill's corps was still north of the James.

Later in the day the two divisions of the VI Corps, which had been despatched by Grant on the 16th, arrived at Bermudah Hundred, and were sent to retake the position lost that morning. But Wright reported that it was doubtful if the line could be carried, and thought that in any case it could not be held in the face of the strong forces advancing from Richmond.

On this day another of Wright's divisions came up on the right of the II Corps, and replaced one of Smith's divisions which was sent to Bermudah Hundred.

On the night of the 17th Beauregard fell back to his ultimate position, which was held till the end of the siege, and was of great strength. It lay behind a ravine, about half a mile from the town.

On the morning of the 18th he was joined by the divisions of Field and Kershaw, and in the afternoon by Hill's corps. Lee arrived in Petersburg about noon.

Fourth Attack on Petersburg, June 18. Grant had ordered a general attack for 4 a.m. on the 18th, but on advancing it was found that the position had been vacated. This necessitated fresh dispositions and the assault was postponed till noon.

The V and IX Corps on the left faced an advanced line of works along the Norfolk railway cut. This was carried after heavy fighting, and late in the afternoon an assault was delivered against the main works beyond, but this was severely repulsed.

In the centre Gibbon's division of the II Corps made an unsuccessful attack at noon, and at 4 p.m. the attack was repeated in stronger force, but with the same fortune. On the right Martindale's two divisions of the XVIII Corps captured the rifle pits of the skirmishing line, but he also could make no impression on the main defences.

It was now evident to Grant that he was again faced by the Army of Virginia, and he ordered the troops to be withdrawn, and put under cover for a much-needed rest.

From the 15th to the 18th the Federal losses were about 10,000, while those of the defenders probably did not amount to half that number.

Causes of Grant's Failure at Petersburg. Grant's design on Petersburg had deserved better success. The transfer of the army of the Potomac to the south of the

PETERSBURG

James was well planned and admirably carried out. The movement was so well executed that Lee was entirely misled.

The failure to capture the town by Smith's surprise assault is attributable to several causes besides the difficulties which always attend such movements. Smith attacked late and Hancock arrived later still. Had they been able to attack together, or had Smith possessed more of the disposition of Hancock, the town would probably have fallen. There was, moreover, a misunderstanding as to Grant's intentions. Hancock had no orders to attack, and only late in the afternoon of the 15th was instructed to "support" Smith.[1] For such an important operation as the seizure of Petersburg, more definite orders should certainly have been issued.

So it happened that on the 15th 14,000 troops of the XVIII Corps, backed by as many more of the II Corps, failed to dislodge the defenders of the town, of whom only 4,400 were regular troops.

Although the opportunity of taking Petersburg by surprise passed on the 15th, there was on the 16th and 17th a good chance of effecting its capture by force.

On the 16th the IX and II and XVIII Corps were opposed by 14,000 Confederates, consisting of the Peters-

---

[1] Meade reported: "Had General Hancock and myself been apprised of the contemplated movement against Petersburg I am of opinion they could have pushed on much earlier." Hancock wrote: "The messages which I received between 5 and 6 p.m. on the 15th were the first and only intimation I had that Petersburg was to be attacked that day."

burg garrison and the divisions of Hoke and Johnson. On both days the division of Gilmore was also at hand in Bermudah Hundred.

On the 17th the four corps of the army of the Potomac together with Butler's force, which was nearly two corps more, failed to overcome the' same small garrison, and yielded the advantage at Bermudah Hundred to Pickett's division of Anderson's corps.

On the morning of the 18th these six Federal Corps were held in check by Beauregard and Anderson; Hill only arriving to repel the afternoon assaults.

The truth was that the Confederacy was reaping the fruits of the magnificent valour of its soldiers in the immediate past. After a week of gallant assaults, fruitless of everything save slaughter, the Federal troops had come to anticipate repulse. With some reason they had begun to regard Lee's parapets as impregnable, and indeed they proved to be so, for until the end, nearly a year later, they held out against all direct assaults, and only fell when the superior number of the Federal army enabled Grant eventually to overlap and turn their flank. The spirit with which Grant had imbued his army, and which had inspired the charges at Spottsylvania and Cold Harbour had broken itself against the steadfast courage of the army of Virginia.

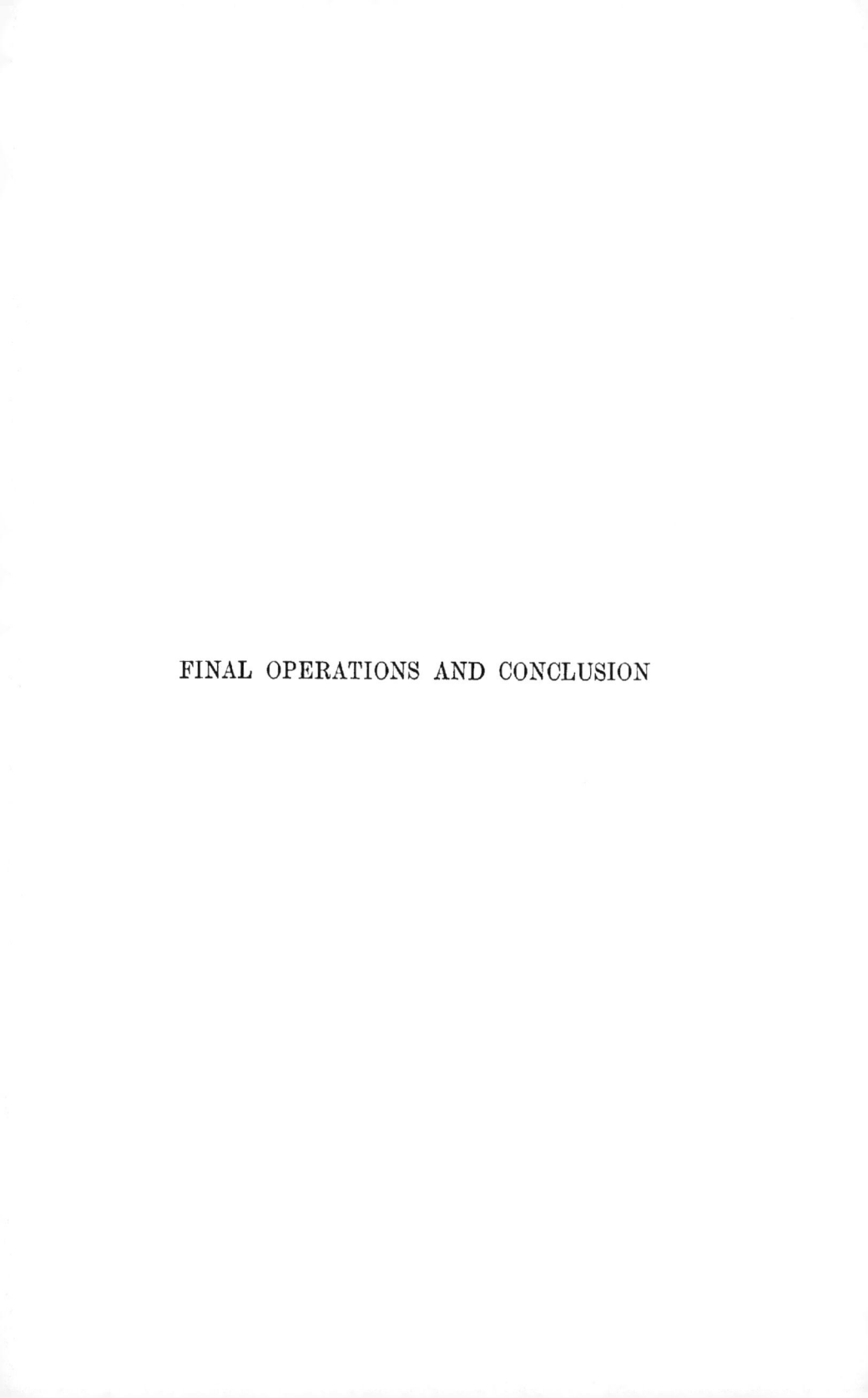

FINAL OPERATIONS AND CONCLUSION

CHAPTER XII

FINAL OPERATIONS AND CONCLUSION

THE repulses before Petersburg and the disheartenment of the troops revealed thereby, convinced Grant of the futility of further general assaults. He now determined to reduce the place by cutting off its connexion with the south. The loss of Petersburg would deprive Richmond of all but one line of communication with the main territory of the Confederacy. In that event this last line (the Danville Railway) could not long have been maintained, and the capital must have been evacuated.

The troops were set to work on the lines of investment on the east, and these were heavily fortified so as to enable them to be held by a small proportion of the army while the main force was being pushed westwards across the two railways leading into the town from the south.

These were the Weldon and Southside lines. The first led due south to the Carolinas, and lay only three miles west of the Jerusalem Plank Road, to which the Federal left already extended. The second ran to Lynchburg, but intersecting the Danville Railway at Burkesville Junction, served also as a communication with Georgia.

The Norfolk line was already in possession of the Federals.

Movement against Weldon Railway, June 22. On the 22nd the VI and II Corps were ordered to move upon the Weldon Railway, and if possible to reach the Southside line and the Appomatox River. The result proved the scheme to be over ambitious.

That morning Birney, in command of the II Corps, moved upon the Jerusalem Plank Road with the VI Corps on his left. It was intended that they should form a continuous line of advance, but the ground was found to be obstructed by jungle and thickets to an extent that made close co-operation impossible. The commanders of the two corps were therefore ordered to act independently, and to defend their own flanks. During the advance the VI Corps proceeded somewhat to the left of the general line, so that a considerable gap existed between the two corps.

To oppose this movement Lee dispatched Hill with the two divisions of Wilcox and Mahone, while B. R. Johnson moved in support. Wilcox met the VI Corps and checked it on the railway, and Mahone fell upon the exposed left of the II Corps.

Barlow's division, which was moving to connect

FINAL OPERATIONS AND CONCLUSION

with the VI Corps, was completely rolled up and suffered severely. At the same time Johnson attacked the right of the II Corps and drove it back, taking four guns. The Federals lost 1,700 prisoners, and the fact that the killed and wounded were few indicates the demoralization into which the troops had fallen.

Both corps fell back to where they had started from, and the VI Corps closed in upon the II Corps. Hill meanwhile had withdrawn to his lines.

Weldon Railway, June 23. At daylight on the 23rd the Federals again advanced. The II Corps reached the point whence they had been driven the day before, and the VI Corps wheeled round on their left across the Jerusalem Plank Road. The advance guards reached the railway and commenced to pull up the track, but the movement of the main body was greatly impeded by the thickets, and consequently slow. During the afternoon Wright reported strong columns of the enemy on his left, although it does not appear that any considerable force was actually there. Meade urged him repeatedly to attack, but Wright failed to comply, and magnified the danger of the situation. As it was approaching nightfall, the VI Corps was withdrawn to the Jerusalem Plank Road in line with the II. This was the last operation in which the Federal infantry was engaged during the month of June.

Simultaneously with this movement Wilson with

his own and Kautz' cavalry divisions started on a raid against the Southside Railway

Wilson's Raid. On the 22nd he crossed the Weldon Railway at Reans Station, and reached the Southside line fourteen miles from Petersburg. He broke up the line as far as Burkesville Junction, and continued the work of destruction to thirty miles southward along the Danville line. At this point he was met by a force of infantry guarding the bridge over the Staunton River, and being unable to proceed further determined to retire.

Throughout his march W. H. Lee's cavalry brigade had hung upon his rear, not being strong enough to interfere with the destruction of the line, but on Sheridian's retirement from his raid against Charlottesville, the whole of the Confederate cavalry were liberated to intercept Wilson.

Wade Hampton's division met him at Stony Creek depôt on the 28th, and defeated his attempt to break through. Wilson then turned northwards to cross the line nearer Petersburg, but was met on the 29th at Reams Station by FitzHugh Lee's division and two brigades of infantry under Mahone, who attacked him and dispersed his force. The scattered regiments by wide detours rejoined the army, but Wilson had lost twelve guns, the whole of his train, and 1,500 men.

On June 21 Sheridan, having reached White House on his return from Charlottesville, was ordered to convoy a train of 900 wagons to the James. He did so successfully, but during the movement on the 25th Gregg's division suffered severely at the hands of Fitz-Hugh's cavalry, which had followed Sheridan.

On the 27th Sheridan was ordered to Reams Station to aid Wilson's return, but arrived too late to afford any assistance.

Here again is to be remarked the pernicious dispersal of the Federal forces which so often led to disaster. With regard to the cavalry it seems often to have been the outcome of mere impatience to do something with that arm. When Wilson started, Sheridan, with Gregg's and Torbert's divisions, was at White House, and the expedition might just as well have waited until it could have been undertaken by the whole Federal cavalry. It would certainly have been opposed by the whole Confederate cavalry, but would have greatly outnumbered it. At Trevylian Station Fitz Hugh Lee and Hampton were unable to defeat Greg and Torbert, and in fact the advantage of the action lay with Sheridan. Had these two divisions been combined with the two divisions of Wilson and Kautz they would only have had the same cavalry opposed to them plus the weak force of W. H. Lee, which proved unequal to interfere with Wilson. There would then have been a good chance of driving the whole Confederate cavalry from the field, and the railway might have been effectually destroyed at leisure.

The Federal losses from May 4 to June 12 are given in official records as under :—

Wilderness, May 5-7	17,666
Spottsylvania, May 8-21	18,399
North Anna and Totopotomoy, May 22-31	3,986
Cold Harbour, June 1-14	12,738
Yellow Tavern	625
Trevylian Station	1,512
Petersburg, June 15-18	9,964
Weldon Railway, June 21	2,000
Stony Creek, June 28	1,500
	68,390

The Confederate losses have never been accurately ascertained, but probably did not exceed 40,000.

In the foregoing chapters certain adverse criticisms have been made upon Grant's conduct of the operations, especially with regard to the subsidiary movements. These must not be taken as an attempt to depreciate the military qualities of that leader. It is impossible to depreciate the facts of his achievements, and it is by these alone that his military qualities can be judged. From the outset of his career he was attended by success. The capture of Forts Henry and Donelson on the Tennessee in February, 1862, was admirably executed, and at the latter place the victory was by no means easily won. Indeed, part of his line suffered severe defeat, and a more vigorous adversary should have turned it to account; but here, as at Shiloh, two month's later, when his whole inc was driven back in confusion from its camps and

FINAL OPERATIONS AND CONCLUSION 193

positions, the adversary did not or was not able to overcome him. In both cases his subordinates and his troops showed a spirit which does not seem to have been present in the Army of the Potomac before Grant's advent to it.

In September and October, 1862, with a reduced force he held his ground against formidable attacks at Iuka and Corinth, and in April, 1863, he defeated and blockaded an army in Vicksburg, maintaining the siege until the fortress was reduced by starvation. On November 24, 1863, having returned from Vicksburg, he completely defeated the main western army of the Confederacy in the great battle of Chattanooga, and from thence was transferred to Virginia to operate against Lee. Here his task was one of great difficulty in spite of his superior numbers, for he was opposed by an army which had not only never suffered actual defeat, but which had already three times attacked and defeated forces nearly as large as those he now disposed, besides having won numerous other victories. The Army of North Virginia was led by a man whose military capacity amounted to genius, and whose exploits had produced an almost superstitious dread in the minds of the Federal commanders. Grant himself remarked upon this apprehension at the Wilderness, when Ewell's attack on the left, late on May 5, reduced certain of his officers to a state of panic. He said, " You seem to think Lee can turn a somersault and land on both flanks and in our rear at the same time," and proceeded to advise them to think less of what the enemy was going to do and more of what they were doing themselves. And yet on more than one occasion Grant himself deferred rather unduly to Lee's reputation for enterprise. (e.g.: In leaving Burnside on the railway on May 4, and in his movement from Spottsylvania; his anxiety for Smith's Corps on May 29 was also hardly justified) This was undoubtedly due partly to his being often "blindfolded" by want of information. In spite of the Federal superiority in cavalry the Southern troopers always succeeded in holding them in check, and only once suffered defeat at their hands. Moreover, the hostility of the inhabitants rendered the collection of intelligence difficult.

Yet in spite of these difficulties and in the face of repulses which would have discouraged most leaders, Grant pressed steadily forward. His determination became communicated to his army, so that not only the spirit of apprehension passed, but even the repulses were interpreted by the soldiers into success as they found themselves ever advancing upon the enemy's capital.

Grant in his first orders to the army declared his objective to be the army of Virginia, and he certainly made it the object of his attack on every possible opportunity, but there is no doubt that he was strongly attracted by Richmond. His instructions to Butler, Crook and Sigel, show that at one time he hoped to defeat Lee west of Richmond, and on this hypothesis criticism has been

FINAL OPERATIONS AND CONCLUSION 195

submitted to the effect that he ought to have fought to a finish in the Wilderness region. But at the same time it may be argued that a more prolonged series of repulses from the same works might have produced a disheartenment on the troops which might have resulted in affording Lee an opportunity for a counterstroke,[1] and it is possible that this consideration may have influenced Grant to push nearer to Richmond in order to give an impression of success to the soldiers.

It is noticeable that while he attacked with the utmost vigour on every occasion, he also showed almost over-caution in his movements from position. This may be put down to the fact that many of his troops were new, and he was well aware that the veterans of Lee's army were superior to them in fighting power as well as in mobility. So this caution seems to have been well reasoned.

But throughout his career Grant does not appear to have been inclined towards brilliant offensive movements such as Lee and Jackson planned and carried out. Possibly he did not think his troops and leaders capable of executing them, but the more probable reason is that he was never under the necessity of adopting these tactics. Lee was always outnumbered, and he was forced to supplement his strength by boldness and rapidity of action. Grant had the strength, and it was obvious that if he could avoid mistakes he must win in the end.

[1] This is what actually happened on June 21, before Petersburg.

So he seems to have preferred the more certain method of striking hard and proceeding cautiously.

He was the first of the Federal generals who proved himself capable of wielding the ponderous weapon of the Potomac army. The others each struck one blow, and when that failed were unable to recover it for a second. Burnside's repulse at Fredericksburg was no worse than Grant's at Spottsylvania; Pope at Manassas was not much worse handled than Grant was at the Wilderness; neither Hooker at Chancellorville nor MacClellan in the Seven Days lost more men than did Grant before Richmond; but, one and all, they immediately acknowledged defeat and promptly yielded the field to the enemy, while in each instance Grant claimed a victory and prepared to push on.

Only the personality of a great leader could have inspired in the army the confidence necessary to do these things. In character he was of an exceedingly amiable and admirable disposition, and considering the immense sacrifice of life he made to gain his ends it is strange to hear that he was extraordinarily affected by the sight of suffering. While he devoted the closest attention to provision for the wounded he could not endure the effect produced by their proximity. It is said that the only occasion throughout the campaign on which he lost his temper was on witnessing a case of cruelty to a horse. With regard to Lee it is difficult to find anything to say but praise.

FINAL OPERATIONS AND CONCLUSION 197

The change from offensive to defensive tactics which was forced upon him by the advent of Grant and the consequent increase in fortitude and vigour of the army of the Potomac, is merely an example of his perception. He entered the Wilderness hoping to win another Chancellorville, but the change in quality of the resistance opposed to him becoming manifest he modified his tactics to meet it, but still he did not abandon the offensive until it became evident that it could no longer command success. The disablement of Longstreet was a heavy loss, but Ewell and Early were both energetic commanders, and each was employed to make an offensive movement against the enemy's flank; the first at Spottsylvania, and the second at Cold Harbour. In both cases Grant's disposition and the steadfastness of his troops defeated the attempts. In the presence of such an adversary Lee was undoubtedly wise not to employ the tactics which proved so effectual against MacClellan, Pope and Hooker, and there can be little doubt that his exceptional mind already realized the hopelessness of the struggle. Jackson and Stuart were gone and with them many of the few who were fighting for independence. There were none to replace them for the resources of the South, both in men and money, were exhausted, and England barred the only hope of freedom.

Nevertheless, he fought on for nearly a year, and his last struggle was a worthy termination of a career to which history affords no parallel.

BIBLIOLIFE

Old Books Deserve a New Life
www.bibliolife.com

Did you know that you can get most of our titles in our trademark **EasyScript**™ print format? **EasyScript**™ provides readers with a larger than average typeface, for a reading experience that's easier on the eyes.

Did you know that we have an ever-growing collection of books in many languages?

Order online:
www.bibliolife.com/store

Or to exclusively browse our **EasyScript**™ collection:
www.bibliogrande.com

At BiblioLife, we aim to make knowledge more accessible by making thousands of titles available to you – quickly and affordably.

Contact us:
BiblioLife
PO Box 21206
Charleston, SC 29413

Printed in Great Britain
by Amazon.co.uk, Ltd.,
Marston Gate.